2012

Y-SIZE YOUR
BUSINESS

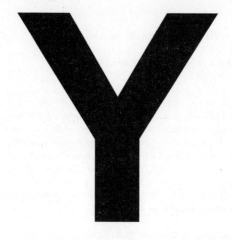

Y-SIZE YOUR
BUSINESS

How **Gen Y Employees** Can Save
You Money and Grow Your Business

JASON RYAN DORSEY

WILEY

John Wiley & Sons, Inc.

Published by John Wiley & Sons, Inc., Hoboken, New Jersey.
Published simultaneously in Canada.

For general information on our other products and services or for technical support, please contact our Customer Care Department within the United States at (800) 762-2974, outside the United States at (317) 572-3993 or fax (317) 572-4002.

Wiley also publishes its books in a variety of electronic formats. Some content that appears in print may not be available in electronic books. For more information about Wiley products, visit our web site at www.wiley.com.

Library of Congress Cataloging-in-Publication Data:

Dorsey, Jason R. (Jason Ryan)
    Y-size your business : how Gen Y employees can save you money and grow your business / by Jason Ryan Dorsey.
        p.   cm.
    Includes index.
    ISBN 978-0-470-50556-4 (cloth)
        1. Personnel management.   2. Young adults—Employment.   3. Generation Y.
    4. Employee motivation.   I. Title.
    HF5549.D575 2010
    658.30084'2—dc22

                                                                    2009037057

Printed in the United States of America
10 9 8 7 6

*This book is dedicated to my wife, Denise,
my favorite Gen Xer. I will never forget when
you thought something was wrong with your cell
phone . . . and it was actually notifying
you of your first text message.
I luv u.* ☺

CONTENTS

CHAPTER 1

Hiring Gen Y Makes Dollars and Sense

(Or, Why a 22-year-old with three tattoos who still lives with his mom could make a fantastic employee . . .)

"WHY SHOULD I HIRE YOUR GENERATION?"

Employers ask me this question almost every day. Then they start in with their stories about "people my age." Two of my recent favorites: "I know all about employing your generation. Last year I hired a young guy right out of college. He had good grades and seemed like a hard worker. A week later I'm in the company bathroom and I hear him talking on his cell phone *in a restroom stall.* And his phone was on speaker! Even worse, he didn't think he was doing anything wrong. He just kept talking and talking."

Or, "I gave a 24-year-old woman her annual performance review last week, and she cried right in front of me! I couldn't believe it. Here I was, a woman who had worked hard to climb the corporate ladder over 20 years, starting at a time when being a woman in the corporate world was hard enough, and here she was, crying on the other side of my desk because she got a good, but not perfect, review. Next thing I know, her mom's on the phone asking to speak to my boss! What is going on with you people? How am I ever going to build a business with your generation as employees?"

Okay, I get it. My peers and I can be a *little* different when we enter the workplace (which is, on average, about 10 minutes later than you'd like). Sure, we show up to work with our iPod buds dangling out of our purse or backpack, and our ever-present cell phone is ringing loudly during the CEO's Monday morning pep talk. Yes, many of us have a tattoo (or several); some of us sport nontraditional hair colors; and it's not uncommon for us to have a piercing somewhere besides our ear lobes (and, no, it doesn't hurt *much*).

However, in my work consulting and speaking with business leaders around the world, I've seen time and again that Gen Y can deliver tremendous workplace performance and loyalty at a substantial value—*when managed correctly*. This combination could not have come at a better time, because the current economic climate is forcing companies to do more with less in an increasingly competitive business environment. It's my belief—and I've seen it in action—that Gen Y can be the strategic differentiator you've been looking for.

My interview with Tad, 25, is one example of the kind of value Gen Y can bring to the workplace. Tad graduated from college and went to work for Intuit, where he was placed in a Rotational Development Program. (I talk about creating these types of programs in Chapter 11.) Part of Intuit's culture is to ask employees to spend 10 percent of their time thinking about ways to better the company or themselves. Tad was part of a group that was trying to come up with a new idea when they realized the area where Intuit could use help was the actual *process of innovation* within the company.

Tackling institutional innovation is a monumental task for an executive of any age, let alone a Gen Yer in his first year of employment at a large company. Undeterred, or possibly too young to know better, Tad and four of his Gen Y coworkers went to work fixing the process of innovation during their "better-themselves-or-the-company" time. He also worked well past midnight and many weekends without any additional pay—something bosses who haven't had good experiences employing Gen Y consider impossible, or simply unbelievable.

A year after his initial idea, and *hundreds* of unpaid hours later, Tad and his coworkers, together with several other employees he inspired to champion the cause, released Intuit Brainstorm, a product that has completely changed innovation at Intuit. In the six months after the new technology's release, ideation at Intuit—meaning the rate of idea creation and advancement within the company—has increased 1,000 percent. Participation by employees in innovation has increased 500 percent, and new ideas have gone from concept to customer demo in as little time as three months—exceptional (and valuable) for a company as large as Intuit. Most impressive, other companies are now licensing Intuit Brainstorm for their own innovation processes, all because a 25-year-old Gen Yer wasn't satisfied with something that was a cornerstone of his company for *years*.

I asked Tad why he would go so far beyond his normal job description to pursue such a farfetched idea. His response: "I just wanted to make the company better. I thought that if I could make innovation easier and more fun, then more people would want to do it."

Before you think Tad is the exception to the rule, or that high-tech innovation doesn't apply in your business, consider the view of Jamie Yarrow, president of Terra Resort Group, who has 500 employees at his hotels, the vast majority of whom are in Gen Y:

> Anyone who says Gen Y is lazy, unmotivated, or can't be a professional, simply doesn't get Gen Y. Sure, they do some things different, but when you figure out where they're coming from, you realize they are really driven to make an impact. The difference in the workplace is *how* they might try to make that impact.

> As an executive, one of the things I value most about my Gen Y employees is that they don't care how good I was last year or last month. They want to know what I'm doing *today* that is going to move the business forward. They never give me a chance to settle

for "good enough." And I'm not saying it's only my Gen Y managers who challenge me, I mean the Gen Yer who is painting my door wants to know how we are going to grow the business.

I can see where some executives would find this offensive, but to me it is a huge *competitive advantage*. They want me to get better every day—so they can get better every day. That kind of focus on ongoing improvement can build a business that is hard to beat.

While I've seen over and over that Gen Y employees can deliver strong performance with the right type of management and leadership, I also know there is a growing generation gap in the workforce that is frustrating employees of all ages. Making the generation gap more extreme, older workers are now delaying retirement, and many who had retired are back looking for jobs. The result is that several of my clients report they have *the largest age gap they've ever had* between their oldest and youngest employees—in some cases the age gap is more than 60 years!

I saw this age gap in action when I was keynoting a conference for executives of large companies in the Midwest. I asked the room full of executives to raise their hands if they felt Gen Yers have a lot to learn when we first show up to work for them. All the hands quickly went up (along with some supporting—and some unrepeatable—comments). Then I asked the executives if they, too, had much to learn at their first job. Again, all the hands went up (with some comments like, "Sure, but I started working when I was 12"). Then I gave them the dream new-hire scenario: "I want you to imagine that a member of my generation, Gen Y, has shown up to work for you. It's our first real job, *so we're probably . . . 24*. We're excited, we're nervous, we're late. If you could give us one piece of advice based on all the lessons you've learned about work since your first job, what would you tell us in one sentence?" Hands shot up again, but the oldest gentleman in the room, who I later learned was in his late 70s, made sure he got my attention. I asked him, "What advice would you give that Gen Yer on our first day of work, at our first real job, that will guide us for the rest of our career?!"

"Pull up your pants!" he shouted. I almost fell off the stage. The entire room burst into laughter, agreement, and applause. Good thing I was wearing a suit and not the jeans I had on the day before . . .

THE GENERATION GAP IS BIGGER
THAN OUR BAGGY PANTS

Anyone who has spent five minutes working in a company alongside Gen Y employees, whom I define as being born between 1977 and 1995 (more on why in Chapter 2), knows we bring different personalities and priorities to the workplace. Some of Gen Y's characteristics can add immediate value to an employer (such as text messaging one-handed while driving—ideal for pizza delivery), while others can be downright confusing or annoying ("Can't you write an e-mail with at least one complete sentence?!"). I often hear employers say, "What's so hard about showing up on time, turning off your cell phone, tucking in your shirt, rolling up your sleeves, and going to work? That's what I did." Clearly the person who says this still has a land line (i.e., home phone) and probably can do magic tricks with a pen, like balance their checkbook *by hand*. But I get where they're coming from.

The attitude, behaviors, and values gap between Gen Y and other generations—the newest generation gap—shows up in all manner of workplace areas, including differences in communication style ("My boss gives me notes in cursive. *I can't read cursive.*"), professionalism ("A tie? Where do I get a tie?"), punctuality (10 minutes early versus well, showing up before lunch), and my favorite, customer service ("You want *me* to count your change back to you? Can't you count?").

While this divide can sometimes be comical to outside observers (unless it's your change we can't seem to count back), it is an absolute crisis in companies that are competing in a global marketplace during incredibly difficult times. This is especially true at companies reliant on Gen Y employees with specialized skills and high starting salaries, such as healthcare or high tech, those with much lower salaries but historically high turnover, such as QSR (fast food) and hospitality, and companies facing an impending retirement bubble or with ambitious growth plans.

HOW I ACCIDENTALLY BECAME
THE GEN Y GUY

As a member of Gen Y who sleeps with his cell phone (really) and a business owner since age 18, I was pulled into bridging this growing generational gap by accident. On one hand, I was speaking and consulting with executives, managers, and entrepreneurs on how to get their Gen Y employees to perform at a higher level and stick around longer without paying us more money (and especially without coddling us). On the other hand, my Gen Y career advice books are estimated to have helped more than 100,000 Gen Yers enter the workforce. I've also personally spoken to more than 500,000 of my peers, representing all 50 states and more than 100 different countries, on how to make the transition into the workplace and the real world.

With this unique vantage point, I was caught smack in the middle of the generational divide. I had unfiltered access to the pressures top business leaders were facing to make the most of Gen Y employees. I also saw the limitations on what business leaders could actually do, given market and operational realities ("No, not all employees get their own computers; we are a cleaning company, after all"). At the same time, Gen Y employees were reading my books, attending my seminars, and then e-mailing me about how "out of touch" their employers were—*the exact same thing* the employers were saying from the other side of their mahogany desks. Clearly there was a growing divide and *everyone* was losing.

I knew there had to be a middle ground that everyone could build on, so I went in search of it. I didn't stop searching until I discovered the solution (more on that journey in Chapter 4). The result of my search is the *Y-Size* process, which is more than just a few steps on how to best employ Gen Y. This process reveals *how employers can make the most of Gen Y while at the same time respecting and incorporating the strengths of the other generations in the same workplace.* The bottom line: Employees of all ages benefit; no one gets coddled; and companies move ahead faster.

EACH NEW GENERATION ENTERS THE WORKPLACE "THE HARD WAY"

To be fair, the generational disconnect (and head shaking) that many employers are experiencing with Gen Y is not unprecedented. In fact, it's pretty standard. Every new generation that enters the workforce causes stress, frustration, and criticism from the generations already employed. Experienced managers and executives believe the younger "kids" (who might be in their late 20s) need to pay their dues "the same way they did." They also believe the new generation had it easier than they did growing up (Okay, I'll admit that you actually suffered through dial-up). At the same time, I've never found a company that did everything right when it came to employing Gen Y *or any other generation*, for that matter.

From an employee perspective, all the executives, managers, and entrepreneurs I have interviewed said they had much to learn when they landed their first real job. Gen Y is no different, except we are entering the workforce later in life, with much less (if any) real world experience, and with even less formal training or preparation. We've also been told by our well-meaning parents (and reinforced by society) that if we can dream it, we can achieve it. Talk about a setup for a knockdown, especially in this economy. Sure, you can be CEO, *but not in the first month*, and, by the way, you start out in the mailroom. And yes, that's mail with stamps.

Although every new generation causes friction and stress in the workplace, there are three factors converging on our current workforce that are extraordinary—factors that are radically raising the stakes for companies to figure out how to best employ Gen Y. These are also the factors that add urgency and weight to the payoff for leading your company through the *Y-Size* process.

1. The economic downturn now affecting the national and global economy

It seems few industries or geographies are immune. Storied companies such as General Motors are filing for bankruptcy or seeking government intervention. Credit is expensive or nonexistent (even if you pay on time!). Revenue and profit margins have been replaced by losses and resignations. Flat is the new growth. As employers look to reduce costs, they are paying close attention to one specific line item: employee costs. At many companies, employee costs are the largest or second largest operational expense. In determining how to maximize the return on their employee investment, executives and CFOs are finding that the numbers don't lie: *Gen Y is often the least expensive employee to hire, especially when you factor in benefits.* On the other hand, Gen Y also brings many skills, albeit in need of refinement, that can be valuable right away, with a little instruction. (See Chapter 11 on how to do this in less than 30 minutes.) And there are a lot of us:

Numbering 79.8 million in the United States, Gen Y is also the fastest growing generation in the workforce. The same situation is true in many other countries.

Talk about a generation being at the right place at the right time! Combine all these factors together and you can't miss the potential return on investment from effectively employing my generation. In my view, Gen Y's emergence in the workforce is a huge strategic opportunity for an employer to create short-term gains as well as position themselves for a long-term competitive advantage *if they know how to employ us*. That's what the *Y-Size* process is all about.

2. Gen Y's fundamentally different attitude toward work

Gen Y is the first generation to enter the current workforce without any expectation of lifetime employment. We have never expected to work for one company for 40 years and retire with a 401k (Good thing, because we think a 401k is a painfully slow Internet connection). Once Gen Y has job options, which will happen when the economy ultimately improves or our workplace skill set develops, our generational viewpoint will also make us more inclined to leave an employer where we don't feel we fit. (However, don't worry: I show you exactly how to retain Gen Y with little extra effort or cost in Chapters 13 and 14.) While on the surface this may seem like Gen Y is born to be disloyal, the opposite is actually true. We are intensely loyal, to the point where we will take a *pay cut* to help an employer we believe in. That said, earning our loyalty means doing a few things differently, but none of these things requires paying us more, and each of these is described later in this book.

3. The multigenerational collision happening in the workplace

These collisions, or disconnects, have reached an unprecedented level because *for the first time ever four distinctly different generations are working side by side*. This has never happened in the modern workforce, and it is creating all kinds of new and unexpected problems. Companies with a four-generation workforce will likely see disconnects (and possibly straight-up conflicts) in communication, motivation, innovation, teamwork, engagement, professionalism, customer service, and leadership. If companies do not bridge these generations and embrace their newest generation of frontline employees, their operating costs will go up, their effectiveness will decrease, and both morale and profits will suffer (although anonymous blog postings will go through the roof).

On the other hand, if companies can successfully navigate the dynamics of a multigenerational workforce, in particular Gen Y's tidal wave-like entry, they can unlock tremendous workplace potential where other companies only unlock infighting. This will become even more valuable when the 80 million Baby Boomers in the United States eventually transition into retirement or more lifestyle-friendly jobs (which has been delayed due to the economy and their 28-year-old son with a master's degree moving home to "find himself"—by playing online poker).

These three converging factors—the economy, Gen Y's workplace attitude, and a multigenerational workforce—underscore the importance of making the most of Gen Y's emergence during a pivotal time for business competition. Adding to a sense of urgency in the United States, our economy is increasingly dominated by service and knowledge industries. By their very nature, these industries depend on younger workers to open doors (literally), answer questions, and shape the customer experience. This is important because at the most expensive service- and knowledge-based companies—whether boutique hotels or highbrow law firms—the first and last person a customer encounters is often a member of Gen Y. This means members of my generation are literally the bookends of the entire customer experience, and some of us don't even own books!

DON'T CATER TO GEN Y—LEAD US

I think it's important to clarify up front that I am 100 percent opposed to catering to my generation's every whim (after all, who really needs a company car in New York City?). In fact, businesses that coddle Gen Y end up attracting the wrong kind of Gen Y employees (the kind who quit without notice and then ask for a job reference). You don't want employees seeking to be coddled and catered to. You want employees seeking to make an impact from Day One, employees who are motivated to prove their potential and show how wise you were to give them a chance. The latter are the employees the *Y-Size* process attracts, retains, and develops.

I believe that with the right insight, and a small amount of effort at key employee life cycle moments, employers can easily find a common ground that benefits them and makes the most of their Gen Y employees. This belief is the backbone of my *Y-Size* process, which is inexpensive to implement, easy to customize, and leads to *measurable results*. The secret is to balance larger Gen Y employment strategies with tactical actions so that every business leader recognizes that they can do something *today* to help make Gen Y a cost-effective, highly productive employee group.

GEN Y ROI

When it comes to the bottom line of your business, Gen Y's emergence could not have come at a better time. Companies must compete to win based on price or quality—or risk going out of business. You want to be Wal-Mart or Nordstrom's, but definitely not Mervyn's. Being flexible to compete on price or quality or both will ultimately trump more bureaucratic competitors, who can only watch the change happening around them and ask for a memo (and probably a PowerPoint summary). Employers also have realized—and are telling me—that despite the fact that unemployment is at a 25-year high, good, reliable, affordable employees remain hard to come by, and they are more valuable than ever because employers have to do more with fewer resources.

Here's the good news: If you've picked up this book, you realize that Gen Y is an opportunity masquerading as a problem (albeit a problem with big expectations). I'm here to help you find the opportunity within the problem, to leverage it strategically and tactically, and to do so while saving you money and growing your business. Before I share my *Y-Size* process, it's essential to dive a little deeper into who Gen Y is and what we are thinking (especially when we got that tattoo at 4 AM). These insights in the next few chapters will help you to see why and how the *Y-Size* process will benefit you as a business leader and your company as a market leader.

Y-SIZE QUESTIONS

1. Do you depend on Gen Y employees for the successful operation of your business?
2. Is your company experiencing difficulties with employees in Gen Y?
3. What one thing would you like to see your Gen Y employees do better?

CHAPTER 2

Behind the Scenes (and Screen Names) with Gen Y

(Or, What we're really thinking when you call five times and we don't answer, but you send a text and we instantly reply.)

I was born on May 30, 1978. I felt I should start by sharing my birthday, since, in true Gen Y style, it's my favorite national holiday. From a research standpoint, I'm on the leading edge of Gen Y in terms of age (more on that in a moment). My experiences growing up at the front of a new generation give me a behind-the-scenes perspective on our beliefs, values, attitudes, expectations, and generation-defining moments—as well as an up close and personal view on how these characteristics do and don't mesh with other generations in the workplace.

As a kid (which some well-meaning older clients still call me), one of my most vivid memories is watching the Challenger Space Shuttle tragedy live on TV in elementary school. This event was Gen Y's first generation-defining moment. I also remember the excitement of receiving my first e-mail—and the annoyance of the 100,000 spam e-mails to follow. And, *yes*, I'll admit, I text message my mom *every* day (*okay*, at least five times a day).

A MEMBER OF GEN Y AND A RESEARCHER OF GEN Y

While being a member of Gen Y certainly gives me a firsthand perspective into our world view (and accompanying core beliefs—such as Wii versus Xbox), it in no way makes me a generational expert. To develop and refine my expertise on Gen Y, I've spent the last five years researching and interviewing Gen Y—and our employers—to understand how we approach work and our entry into the real world. I've discovered that, as a generation, despite our sometimes wildly different clothing styles, accents, and favorite shows to DVR, Gen Y is in many ways *amazingly consistent* across the United States—and to some degree internationally. Whether I was meeting with Gen Yers in Juneau, Alaska; Miami, Florida; or Lincoln, Nebraska, the same generational beliefs, values, preferences, and priorities emerged (although the accents and the coffee were much different).

My time interviewing, speaking to, researching, and working with Gen Y has helped me to understand the big picture of who we are and the reasons behind the potential we bring to the workplace—as well as the "issues" we can create once employed. One benefit of being in Gen Y is that the Gen Yers I met with saw me as a peer, so they felt comfortable opening up with some of their most deeply held beliefs (and a few comments that might make their parents cringe, or at least take back their "emergency-only" credit card).

HOW DO WE DEFINE A GENERATION?

I define a generation as a segment of a geographically linked population that experienced similar social and cultural events at roughly the same time in their maturation. Yes, that's a mouthful, but all you really need to know is that *a generation is a group of people born at about the same time and raised in about the same place*. That's it. We can use all kinds of fancy words, but at the end of the day, that's what it is.

One important phrase to highlight in the fancy definition is "geographically linked." In my experience speaking and consulting, I've racked up millions of air miles (and way too many delays at O'Hare). In doing so, I've learned that people in the same generation have different perspectives based on where they grew up. You will see differences in perspectives when you talk with people in the same generation from a small town versus a big city or within the United States versus other countries. Recognizing the importance geography can play in shaping a generation keeps us mindful that the more similar your employees' geographic background, the more likely they will exhibit similar workplace behaviors within a specific generation.

MEMBERS OF THE SAME GENERATION CAN COME FROM DIFFERENT WORLDS

My best friend and I are good examples of the role geography can play in influencing those within the same generation. He and I are very close in age, but he grew up on the outskirts of New York City, and I grew up in the outskirts of a cow pasture (really, you have to go over a cattle guard to get up my driveway). My best friend went to school with people from 40 different countries, heard multiple languages spoken every day, could eat at any type of restaurant imaginable, and visit a multitude of museums—although proximity alone doesn't guarantee he went (that's cultural). I, on the other hand, went to a school where maybe two or three different languages were spoken (if you include "Texan" as one of the options), and as a kid I would get dressed up to go to Wal-Mart because it was always a "spontaneous family reunion."

My point is this: A generation is not a rigid box that every single person of a certain age will fit neatly inside. Rather, I see generational identity as simply a clue—*a big clue*—about where to start to more effectively connect with, engage, and lead people of different ages. A clue—*not a box*. I don't look at a Baby Boomer across the room and think "Ha! Boomer! You get to work early, you stay late, you tuck in your shirt, and you work on weekends!" Okay, *so that's all true*, but my work has taught me that, by their very nature, generations have to be defined broadly. If I listed enough characteristics about any one generation, including my own, no one reading this book would fit all of them (not even me).

That said, I have found tremendous value and immediate results when applying my studies of different generations to the workplace. These techniques help me to teach people of different ages to work together better, faster, and with fewer resources. These studies also identify the common ground we can all build on to strengthen our cross-generational relationships and to improve our performance at work.

GENERATION-DEFINING MOMENTS—WHERE A GENERATION COMES TOGETHER

Determining where one generation ends and a new one begins can be argued as both art or science. Ask five different generational experts and you'll likely get five different answers. My approach is to focus on the generation-defining moments that serve as the bookends for a generation's experience. These are the moments that bring an entire generation together, one event at a time, and ultimately create a through-line for our most formative experiences.

There are several that stand out with Gen Y. The first one is the Challenger tragedy, which the oldest Gen Yers, like myself, watched during elementary school in 1986. I remember watching the shuttle roar into the sky and then feeling the pain when I realized what had just happened. The next event was the fall of the Berlin Wall in 1989 (we heard the wall fall but we didn't know where Berlin was on a map—and some of us still don't), followed by the Gulf War in the early 1990s (which we watched live on TV from the comfort of our home). After that you get into more pop culture influences (You go, Britney!). The capstone event for us is September 11, 2001.

9/11 is my generation's JFK assassination. It is our "Where were you when . . . ?" moment. I will never forget where I was: Los Angeles. I got stranded in L.A. with my father for three days. All commercial flights were grounded, and we watched fighter jets circle the city. I will never forget it for the rest of my life. Using the Challenger tragedy and 9/11 events as bookends, you end up with the approximate birth years 1977 to 1995 to define Gen Y, because *you have to be old enough to emotionally and logically process the significance of an event for it to shape you starting from the moment it occurs.* Some people argue that Gen Y goes all the way to the birth year 2000, but I don't see how that is possible. If you were born after 1995, it would be extremely difficult, if not impossible, to process the significance of September 11th. In fact, if you had little kids at home at the time, the news media told you to turn off the TV.

STATISTICALLY, GEN Y IS ALMOST 80 MILLION STRONG

Relying on the birth years 1977 to 1995, Gen Y, my generation, numbers almost 80 million strong in the United States. This would make us the fastest growing demographic in the U.S. workforce. Outside the United States, depending on birth rates and other demographic factors, Gen Y may also be the fastest growing generation in the workforce. If we are not, it only means that Gen Y is even more important to effectively attract, retain, and develop because there are proportionally fewer of us to employ. *Knowing and understanding what makes Gen Y different in the workplace is the secret to determining the strategies and actions that can transform us into high-performing employees.*

My research shows that Gen Y has 10 defining workplace characteristics, our own Top 10 List for how we think and act at work. These 10 characteristics will highlight the areas where Gen Y is most similar (and most different) from your own generation—besides thinking that being 10 minutes late to work is still "on time."

Late-night talk show drum roll, please . . .

GEN Y'S TOP TEN LIST FOR HOW WE THINK AND ACT AT WORK

1. No expectation of lifetime employment

Gen Y is the *only* generation in the modern workforce that has *never* expected to work for one employer for our entire career. In practice this means that Gen Y *expects* to change employers throughout our lives, because it would be *abnormal* for us to stay with one company. This doesn't mean Gen Y won't or can't stay with one employer, just that we see nothing wrong with switching employers if a job or company no longer fits us (or our sleep schedule).

How often is Gen Y willing to change? This depends upon our long-term commitments, age, and the economy, but there is one big difference. My interviews with Gen Y reveal that on average we define long-term employment, being a "loyal" employee, as working at the same company for 13 months (and that's using all our vacation days). If we get to the end of the year and we have vacation days left, we miscounted. This means Gen Y has a fundamentally different belief about the employer-employee relationship that is in direct conflict with other employee generations. The bottom line: We have *never* thought we would work somewhere for 40 years, retire, and get a watch and a plaque and a cake. Good thing, because we don't wear watches, our mom would have to hang up the plaque, and we prefer locally sourced organic desserts. In fact, when it comes to our careers, some in Gen Y view staying in one job or even with one company for more than five years as indicating our career has *stalled*.

When I asked Gen Y about loyalty I also learned one critical but often-overlooked fact: *Gen Y does not define loyalty as being measured by tenure;* that's a characteristic of older generations. In fact, many in Gen Y would view ourselves as being *disloyal* to our employer if we stayed at a job we didn't like or were no longer passionate about. We actually think it is being *loyal to an employer* if we quit when we are no longer excited about our job or the company. Maybe that's why we can't seem to give one week's notice . . .

How does Gen Y define loyalty? *Effort.* It's not *how long* we worked somewhere, but *how hard we worked* while we were there. This is how we can ask you for a job reference after only working at your business for three months. After all, we worked "really hard" the entire time.

Though we may not expect to be with a company for 20 years, we are willing to work extremely long hours for an employer *if we feel a genuine connection to the company or its mission.* At one online education company I visited, the Gen Y employees were working seven days a week, and some were taking showers in the office building in order to meet deadlines (and maintain some standard of hygiene). One of the Gen Y employees told me, "That's just what you do when your company is counting on you."

The key is to *align company goals with Gen Y's personal goals*, and by that I mean finding ways to show Gen Y how we can reach our personal goals at the same time we are achieving company goals. If working long hours for eight weeks eventually means we get two Fridays off from work, we're all yours. At this particular company, they celebrated meeting their deadline by closing the business the following day (in the middle of the week) and taking all the employees to play sand volleyball, followed by a party where they could invite a friend. I will suggest many more (less sandy ways) to build Gen Y's employee loyalty in Chapter 14.

2. A feeling of entitlement along with big expectations

The biggest complaint I get from employers of all ages—including Gen Yers who manage other Gen Yers—is that many in Gen Y feel entitled. We show up to work and act as if our boss owes us something for our presence. An employer says something like, "So, where do you see yourself in one year?" and Gen Y responds, "In your chair, but I'd buy a better one. I like my chairs to massage *and* recline."

I know how off-putting Gen Y's attitude can be, but before we condemn my generation as a bunch of spoiled brats (something that I find personally offensive and plan to tell my mom about) we should consider for a moment that *entitlement is 100 percent a learned behavior.* You are not born entitled. You have to be raised that way.

Gen Y's parents are mainly Baby Boomers who raised us with a distinct parenting philosophy, which is: "We want it to be easier for our children than it was for us." The problem with saving children from consequences over and over, and then doing everything you can to make their life easier, is that it does not teach them to be self-reliant and independent. It teaches them to be reliant and dependent—and still have big expectations.

Rather than have Gen Y struggle as they themselves did, our Boomer parents swooped in to save us from consequences and tried constantly to make our lives easier—even if it meant they had to work harder (especially once they cosigned on our loans). When a Boomer got in trouble at school, it was nothing, *nothing* compared to what their parents were going to do in the privacy of their home. Gen Y's discipline experience was completely different. On the way to the principal's office we texted our moms: "Bring the attorney, I'm going in!" Please keep in mind this is not a rich thing or a poor thing; this is a parenting thing. Rich kids just have better attorneys.

This might hit a bit close to home if your twentysomething child is still on your car insurance and cell phone plan. In fact, many of us in Gen Y were told, "As long as you're in college, we'll help you out." Seven majors and one study abroad semester later, we're graduating with 196 credit hours and an associate degree— and courageously entering adulthood by returning home. "Thanks for taking me back! Can you wash my car, too?" After all, you're paying for it.

3. A hunger for instant gratification and tangible outcomes

Gen Y has come of age with almost instantaneous access to just about everything and everyone—from instant meals to instant messages. This constant immediacy has taught us to have little patience, short attention spans, and to seek ongoing progress in every aspect of our life. We hate waiting in lines at the grocery store (Can you say self checkout?) and don't want to show our work on math problems, especially if you already told us our answer is correct. We will even walk into a coffee shop, see a line at the counter, and leave to go somewhere else (I plead guilty here).

However, rather than brand us as the "instant everything" generation, my research shows we are simply *outcome-driven*. This observation changes the conversation, because it shows we are not about having everything *now*, we simply don't see—and therefore we do not appreciate—the steps involved in creating the outcomes we want. We literally do not connect the dots or consider our plans in terms of policies and procedures—that's an older generation's way of approaching work. Instead, all we want to know is what you want us to do. Then get out of our way so we can get it done. In the workplace, this makes us extremely project-oriented rather than job-description-focused.

The problem with our emphasis on outcomes over steps and status quo is that if we don't see the steps necessary to achieve an outcome, we have trouble valuing the work of people who have already taken those steps (and possibly even paved the way). We don't see the many positions our bosses held before earning their way to VP. We only know that we want to become VP and it's been two months, so why aren't we promoted *yet?* Our inability to see the steps involved to get from where we are to where we want to be is one of the reasons many of us have such big expectations tied to unrealistic timelines. We literally don't see the path—only the oasis at the end and us throwing a pool party.

Since we don't see the steps involved, we also end up challenging the status quo, sometimes inadvertently, because we can't see it in the first place (after all, we don't actually read memos, they are strictly for recycling). Our ability to not be limited by traditional paths and solutions has the potential to make us good at problem solving. But our lack of respect for established processes and protocols poses a risk, because these boundaries are real-world guardrails for ensuring quality, safety, and consistency in a company's operations.

4. A new relationship with technology and communication

Since Gen Y grew up during the Internet boom and the mobile communication revolution, technology has become an extension of ourselves. However, older generations have a big misconception when it comes to Gen Y and technology. Older generations think that Gen Y is tech savvy. This is 100 percent not true. Gen Y is not tech savvy, *we are tech dependent.* Important difference. We don't know how technology works. We just know we can't live without it.

How dependent are we on technology? I asked a college recruiter how she was marketing her college differently now than in the past to catch Gen Y's attention. She said she was heavily promoting her college's new dorm washing machines. I said, "What are you talking about?" She said, "Jason, you don't understand. Our new washing machines send you a text message when your laundry is done." Now that is genius! I can never tell when my towels are dry.

With Gen Y's dependence on technology, it is no wonder we expect instant access to information and state-of-the-art entertainment all the time—and largely for free (even on airplanes). We are used to having overwhelming choices and on-demand products and programming 24 hours a day, seven days a week, no matter where we are, and without commercials, thank you. We also expect to stay in constant contact with friends, coworkers, and family members around the clock. Unfortunately, I've observed that Gen Y's dependence on technology has come with a tradeoff, and that tradeoff is our interpersonal communication skills, especially when talking in person with older adults.

One of my clients told me that his daughter called him to say she had just broken up with her boyfriend by text message. My client, who is a Boomer executive, said in a fatherly way that she was being rude to break up with the young man like that. She said, "What do you mean? That's how he asked me out!"

Some people, such as our parents, see us using multiple technology devices at once and think we must be great multitaskers. Wrong. We find comfort (but not efficiency) having multiple tech devices spewing content all at once. We feel safe texting our friends, watching TV, surfing the Web, and listening to streaming music—all while doing our homework. The truth is that many Gen Yers are bad at multitasking. We are easily distracted and simply find comfort amidst the stimulation of lots of things happening all around us at once.

A Gen Y executive at a major retailer told it to me this way, "I have six half-written e-mails open on my computer right now; I'm texting two people; I'm IMing three people; Twitter feeds are coming in; I'm on my cell phone; music is playing in the background; and people are constantly dropping by my desk to talk with me. I love my job. There is so much action around me I can't help but get work done."

5. A higher tolerance for diversity of all kinds

Gen Y is the most ethnically and racially diverse generation in U.S. history. We have also grown up during a period of unprecedented multiculturalism. The Internet, pop culture, immigration trends, interracial marriages, increasingly diverse schools and colleges, plus increased globalization all contribute to Gen Y's familiarity and comfort with varied groups. Ironically, our comfort with different races and ethnicities can actually lead to situations where we are unintentionally offensive to older generations. The reason: Some of us are so oblivious to seeing race or ethnicity as an issue that we say things not realizing how they can be interpreted by people who do not share a similar worldview. This is in spite of us coming of age in a time of immense political correctness.

On balance, Gen Y's comfort with diversity should be a major plus for employers, because racial and ethnic diversity opens the door to increased cognitive diversity, or diversity of thought. As businesses compete in an increasingly global marketplace, they will need to bring new approaches and new solutions in order to win. Diversity of thought is a proven strategy for approaching and solving old problems in new and different ways.

6. A desire to be our own boss

The appeal to become our own boss is powerful with Gen Y, more so than any other generation in the workplace. My generation glamorizes everything about being an entrepreneur, from the idea of starting your own company with no money in your college dorm room (which is what I did), to having a million-dollar breakthrough idea (which I didn't), to taking the idea from concept to customer, and eventually reaping the financial rewards (all of which culminate in being featured in a Donny Deutsch interview).

Entrepreneurship is especially appealing to Gen Y because we view the lifestyle of an entrepreneur as even more motivating than a financial windfall. (If we were offered the same amount of money, we'd rather have earned it by starting our own company than by winning the lottery). We like the idea of making important decisions, leading a team through chaos, and ultimately earning the big Ernst & Young Entrepreneur of the Year trophy or *Fortune* magazine cover story.

What are we really after? Control of our schedules and the chance to do something we are passionate about. We want to be able to show up late and leave early. We also want to fire ourselves when it's a beautiful day so that we can head to the lake with our unemployed friends. The irony is that any experienced entrepreneur will immediately know how disconnected this perception is from the reality of running your own business. Sure, you can take off work when it's nice outside, but you're also working well after midnight to make up for the lost time you spent hanging out with friends (where you ended up talking about work anyway).

7. Gen Y decides to stay—or not—on our first day at work

You read that correctly: We decide on our *very first day at work* whether or not we are going to stay with an employer long term. In fact, I would argue many of us know by lunch. If by lunch we love our new job, we are texting our friends to apply ASAP. If by lunch we don't like our job, we spend the rest of the day "working," which means surfing the mobile Web looking for a new job while at our current job. One of my clients in the hospitality business says he has a name for what Gen Y does on the first day at work. He calls it "the Bathroom to Nowhere." This is when a Gen Yer shows up for the first day at work, asks to go the bathroom, *and never comes back*. The unprecedented importance of the first day of work to Gen Y new hires can be a tremendous advantage to the employer who knows how to present this experience to Gen Y. I will show you how to create an unforgettable first day for little or no money in Chapter 7.

8. A need for ongoing feedback

When it comes to employing Gen Y, if your company only gives annual reviews, then you can change the name. Call them exit interviews, because Gen Y won't be there.

We need feedback on a much more regular schedule, ideally twice a month. However don't confuse frequency with a major time investment. We don't want an in-depth 360-degree performance review, complete with personality assessment, just a five-second check-in that says you notice we exist. All we need is for you to pause outside our cubicle and say, "Jordan, I saw how you helped Mrs. Booker solve the billing problem. Good job." That's it. Nothing more.

You can think about the interaction we want in terms of a text message versus a multi-page memo (with those outdated things called "paragraphs"). Give us 140 characters, max. Super short. To the point. One way. No fluff. Even an e-mail where you only write to us in the subject line can lift our spirits for an entire week (more about this in Chapters 9 and 12).

9. A lack of real-world expertise

Gen Y is entering the workforce later in life. Some of us are entering up to five years later than Boomers (and that's only because there were no more majors left for us to take in college). By the time we are 22 and getting our first "real" job, our Boomer bosses may have already had three jobs *at the same time* (not to mention two kids). Making our real-world experience gap even worse, career education programs are disappearing in secondary schools and colleges across the country.

The focus on core academics is needed, but for many of us it is coming at the cost of learning how to participate in a business meeting or act like a professional at work (all of which are learned skills). All Gen Y needs to get an educational sneak peek into the real world is an unglamorous part-time job during high school, an internship before we graduate college, or to start work full time. This lack of real-world exposure and experience leads Gen Y to conduct ourselves in a manner that may be viewed by other generations as unprofessional, lazy, or uneducated—even though more of us have college degrees than any previous generation.

My observation: We simply may not know any better. You probably had a lot to learn when you started your first job, and so do we. The difference is you had that first job when you were much younger than we are, so we are starting in the same place, just at a later age (and with more credit card debt). It's fair to assume that Gen Y has some catching up to do in the real-world education department—along with that awful term "growing up." The question is, which company will invest the small amount of time and effort necessary to improve our workplace skills, so they can quickly increase our value without increasing our pay?

10. A habit of putting our lifestyle way ahead of work

Gen Y places great value, and a large part our identity, on what we do and who we are *outside of work*. Whereas a Boomer's identity is mainly driven by what they do from 8 AM to 5 PM (okay, so 7 to 7 plus Saturdays), Gen Y's identity starts after 5 PM (or 4:30 PM on Fridays).

By placing such a big emphasis on our time spent outside of work, we are directly elevating the importance of the social and recreational aspects of our lives. *We are valuing lifestyle and relationships above work.* This explains how we can move to a new city and *then* look for a job. I have met so many Gen Yers who have made exactly this type of move— first, job search, second, decision. While this freaks out our parents (and increases our blog readership), it simply seems normal to us because it matches our values. These values are reinforced every time we're told, "You're only going to be young once, so make the most of it!" Of course we're going to Europe this summer. It's not real money. It's Visa.

I am asked often by executives (and Boomer parents) how Gen Y can afford to stay in a hotel in a city where we don't have a job. That is so funny to me. We don't stay in hotels. We go to www.couchsurfing.com and sign up to sleep on a stranger's couch for free. After all, it has to be safe—it's on the Web.

TURNING THESE GEN Y CHARACTERISTICS INTO A COMPETITIVE ADVANTAGE

As a member of Gen Y, I know that not all of these characteristics appear as potential workplace strengths on first reading (or third, for that matter). However, I have seen time and again how employers have made *every one* of these 10 Gen Y characteristics into a workplace advantage *when Gen Y is managed correctly.*

It's all about anticipating, understanding, and capitalizing on these dominant Gen Y characteristics so that your company can turn this emerging labor force into a force to be reckoned with. *The breakthrough moment for many of my clients is realizing that what Gen Y actually wants from our employer in order to put forth our best effort is not that hard to give.* In fact, it usually is less expensive and easier than their current employment practices, and can be readily aligned to their company's interests.

HELPING GEN Y IS PERSONAL TO ME

As a member of Gen Y, I view our primary influences and generation-defining moments through a highly personal lens. Each triggers a memory (or several), and now that I've talked with thousands of Gen Yers it's fascinating for me to see how a single event or common influence can so deeply impact us in similar ways. These experiences and influences are at the heart of Gen Y's beliefs, values, preferences, and priorities—many of which are different from previous generations (more on that in Chapter 3).

The combination of these beliefs, values, preferences, and priorities leads to the 10 dominant characteristics that Gen Y brings to the workplace. These are the 10 generationally critical characteristics that employers must know and understand—although you certainly don't have to agree with them—if you want to make the most of your Gen Y employees from Day One. These characteristics, and the influences and experiences that created them, are the reasons the *Y-Size* process works. It is specifically designed to connect with Gen Y from the inside out.

Y-SIZE QUESTIONS

1. How old were you when you had your first job? Have you asked your Gen Y employees how old they were?
2. What do you think is the most important piece of technology to Gen Y? What is the most important piece of technology to you?
3. Of the 10 workplace characteristics listed in this chapter, which one is most different from your own? Which one is most similar?

CHAPTER 3

Four Generations, One Workplace, Lots of Issues

(Or, Boomers have all kinds of cool skills my generation doesn't. My favorite: long division.)

Gen Y is not alone in bringing a different attitude and perspective to the workplace. Remember bell-bottom pants, polyester suits, and their accompanying "free spirit" swagger? What about the *Leave It to Beaver* "Corporate Man" attitude that was projected on TV and in smoke-filled offices? When they enter the workplace, *all* new generations carry with them their own set of *beliefs* and *values*, *preferences* and *priorities*. Sometimes these differences work well together (think: Trivial Pursuit teams), and sometimes they simply fail to connect.

You know exactly what I'm talking about if you've ever had an extremely important conversation with a Gen Yer, and at the end of the conversation you watched the person walk away *knowing he or she had absolutely no idea what you just told them.* What does a Boomer manager do? She gets out a pen and paper and writes the Gen Yer a note, by hand—in cursive. *We can't read cursive!* How does Gen Y respond? By sending our boss a text message, which she never gets. This disconnect is going to be either a growing problem or a strategic opportunity, *depending entirely on how you choose to approach it.*

Both generations tried to connect in the way that each felt was most comfortable and effective. *And both failed.* This is why *it's essential for employers to consider Gen Y in the context of the other three generations already at work* if they are to best employ Gen Y and keep the other generations happy. I'll talk more about the characteristics of all four generations later in the chapter, but it is useful to briefly identify them here. The Matures are those born before 1946. The Boomers were born between 1946 and 1964. Generation X, or Gen X, was born between 1965 and 1976. And Gen Y was born between 1977 and 1995.

GENERATIONS WORKING TOGETHER—OR TRYING TO

For the first time in U.S. history, four distinctly different generations are working side by side. This has never happened before, and it explains why business leaders of all experience levels, titles, and degrees are not fully prepared to mesh the varying workplace styles now sharing an office, break room, front desk, cash register, or annual meeting—let alone deal with Gen Y's emergence (and the accompanying onslaught of text messages). The challenge of leading a four-generation workplace is so new that many of the best business schools have only recently added the topic to their standard curriculum. In fact, some MBA programs have yet to add the subject. Why? This situation was simply not supposed to happen.

Matures were supposed to be retired (and working hard to spoil their great-grandkids—Thanks, Grandpa!). Boomers were supposed to be retiring, on the verge of retiring, or at least considering a more lifestyle-friendly career move. Generation X was supposed to be assuming the leadership roles vacated by the Boomers, and Gen Y was supposed

to be smoothly entering the business world ready to make an immediate impact. This logical transition has been turned upside down.

Boomers are living longer than they expected; they're healthier
than they expected; and they are finally in positions of influence in
their organization—which supports their workaholic mentality. At
the same time, their home values have imploded; their stocks and
retirement have plunged; and their grown kids keep calling "for a
little more help." If anything, older workers, such as the Matures, are
reentering the workforce because they feel that financially they have
no choice. Many of my clients report that the age range between
their youngest and oldest employee has never been as large as it is
now and that they expect it to continue to grow.

The impact of four generations working side by side is evident in almost every business operation, from product creation and
internal communication to orientation and outside sales (i.e., moving from door-to-door to Twitter feed). *When generations don't work
well together, operational costs go up and operational effectiveness goes down.*
Companies experience problems ranging from decreased customer
service and product quality issues to information breakdowns, higher
turnover, and lots more stress. When conflict really develops between
the generations, you will find employees unwilling to work in multigenerational teams, or ineffective when doing so. Innovation takes
a back seat to playing it safe, and everyone points fingers at someone else. The resulting tension between coworkers can boil over and
cause more unnecessary problems that lead to new distractions that
company leadership doesn't have time to solve—especially given our
difficult economy.

Most importantly, for you as a business leader, *the challenge and
urgency of leading a multigenerational workforce is only going to grow as the
demographic shift in the workplace accelerates.* Gen Y is already entering the workforce in record numbers. Meanwhile, older workers are
refusing to leave or are returning to the workplace (and trying to
get their kid a job in the process). And if generations do become
shorter in duration, as my research indicates they might, a four-generation workforce will become the new norm. We may even see a
five-generation workforce in the not-too-distant future.

The result is that understanding and effectively leading Gen Y,
alongside the other three generations, will become one of management's *most sought-after skills.* This level of leadership requires awareness

of each generation's defining characteristics, workplace attitudes, beliefs, and communication styles—and where they fit with your own. This is particularly important, since it's rare for a company to only employ Gen Y. In fact, my most popular presentation topic and consulting focus is not limited to Gen Y, but how to embrace Gen Y while making the most of all four generations in the workplace.

To gain the big-picture view of the four generations and how they interact in one workplace, we start by taking a step back to consider what really makes up a generation.

CRITICAL FACTORS THAT SHAPE A GENERATION

There are four factors that most shape a generation. I first learned about these from my friend Cam Marston of Generational Insight, and I have expanded on them based on my research and experience teaching leaders how to bridge the generations. These four factors make generations different from one another, and also give those within the same generation common strengths, weaknesses, beliefs, and biases. These four factors also explain why certain generations get along splendidly in the workplace, and others seem to constantly clash like six-year-olds fighting for the same Wii game console.

Cam Marston has identified four critical factors:

1. *Parenting trends.* How we are raised is the greatest influencer of how we will behave in the workplace.
2. *Technology.* All of us have a different relationship with technology that is primarily driven by our age.
3. *Economics.* Our beliefs about money are forged early in life and impact our workplace decisions.
4. *Life span.* How long we think we have to live affects what we do with the time we believe we have left.

PARENTING TRENDS

To highlight the glaring difference in parenting trends between Gen Y and our Boomer parents, look no further than each of our 18th birthdays. When Boomers turned 18, their moms and their dads met them at the door, because they were married (to each other). Boomers were told, "We love you. We are so proud of you. You have a big future ahead. But you're 18 now, so you need to get *another* job, go to college, join the military, get married, we don't care— get out."

And 80 million Boomers went into the world (some with flowers in their hair) to work in an environment where there were more people than there were jobs—something Gen Y cannot fathom. Boomers also expected to start at the bottom of the organizational chart and work their way up without skipping a level. They knew there were no shortcuts to success except *hard work*. While many Boomers found the transition into the workforce difficult and often unglamorous, they would never move back home (good thing, because their parents would never have them back). The bottom line is that Boomers were raised to believe that they would have to rely on their own efforts and initiative if they were going to get what they wanted from work and life.

Gen Y had a totally different experience when we turned 18. Our moms and our dads met us at the door (they made a joint appearance for the occasion). They hugged us and said, "We love you. We are so proud of you. You have a big future ahead. But you're 18 now . . . so as long as you're in college, we'll help you out." We jumped up and down in our flip flops: *Yes! Yes! Yes!*

So off we went to college, *for six years*, to get an *associate degree*. And when we finally finished, where did over half of all the Gen Yers who actually graduated college immediately go with their cap and gown? Home! And our parents took us back. Because in the United States, Boomers as parents share one defining philosophy, which is: "We want it to be easier for our children than it was for us." The challenge is that their well-intentioned efforts to make life easier for Gen Y ended up with us becoming dependent on them, for everything from doing laundry and balancing finances to setting up a profile for us on Match.com.

In fact, some psychologists are using a new term to describe the behavior of people in their 20s in the United States: adultolescence. This is the stage when a Gen Yer wants all the freedom of being an adult, without any of the responsibilities. When I interview my Gen Y peers to find out when they think that they are "officially" adults, the average response is age 30. *That's, right 30!* This is important because if you don't think you're an adult, you don't have to act like an adult.

ECONOMICS

A second major factor that shapes a generation is economics. The relative wealth of a generation, and the economic cycles affecting its members as they are coming of age, creates a lasting impression on their concept of money: rich, poor, normal, and outrageous. For example, the Matures grew up around the Great Depression. They are consummate savers. They take leftovers home when eating at restaurants and pay cash for *everything*. They also clip coupons, hunt for one-day-only sales, and will drive the same car for 30 years.

Gen Y has had the completely opposite economic experience from the Matures. Gen Y has come of age surrounded by more affluence than any generation in modern U.S. history. Growing up, we were bombarded with zero interest balance transfers, the promise of real estate fortunes with no money down, a skyrocketing stock market that included billion-dollar companies with fake profits, and get-rich-quick Internet businesses that you could start from the comfort of your mom's couch. Gen Y has been pummeled with the idea that success is all about money, and excess spending means extra successful.

And our parents listened. We saw them buy larger houses, nicer cars, and $700 purses (or knock-offs of $700 purses). This lifestyle-forward message of materialism was reinforced at all levels in our society and media. Now we are getting a very different message, and for some of us it is finally hitting home, because our parents are losing their homes. We have now witnessed the dotcom bust, the housing bust, the credit crunch, and mass layoffs at major corporations. We have seen our credit card interest rates go up dramatically when we pay one day late, and if we pay on time our credit limits are decreased. We are trying hard to reconcile what is normal, what is temporary, and why a good cosigner is so hard to come by (let alone marry).

TECHNOLOGY

A third factor is technology. Some experts argue that technology shapes a generation, while others argue that, no, a generation shapes technology. For the purposes of understanding how the four generations interact in your workforce, what matters most is simply recognizing that *all the people in your business have a different relationship with technology that is largely based on their age.* Some of my older audiences remember a computer that took punch cards (and took up half a room), and listening to Aunt Bertha's heavy breathing on a telephone party line. My Boomer audiences remember using a mimeograph machine (and smelling the famous purple paper), while my Gen Xers remember playing Frogger until their fingers were numb and all the logs seemed to be sinking.

Gen Y is no different, except that we are now completely dependent on technology. Gen Y has largely come of age with cell phones as umbilical cords, and everything we need is available to us 24/7 with the push of the right keys. (Good thing, because we don't carry cash.) Since almost all companies are now reliant on technology for their business processes, it is important to understand the relationship between technology and different generations—more specifically the comfort level each generation has with different types of technology.

LIFE SPAN

The fourth factor, and often the most underestimated, is life span. *How long you think you will live influences what you do with the time you believe you have left.* In the workplace, this has most impacted Boomers. They thought by now they would be retired. Instead, they are doing everything they can to keep their job. In terms of reentry into the workforce, the Matures are those who have been most affected. Some I've spoken with had not had a job in 10 or more years but are now forced to seek work because their savings have run out, their government benefits are not enough, and they have too much pride to ask their grown children for help (which works out okay, because their grown children are struggling right now, too).

The combination of these four factors—parenting trends, technology, economics, and life span—together with many other lesser factors, combines to give each generation its unique set of beliefs, values, preferences, priorities, attitudes, expectations, and communication styles. There is also an argument to be made that as the rate of change in these four primary factors quickens, generations could become shorter in duration. This does not automatically mean generations will become smaller in total size. That is a function of population and birth rates. It does mean, however, that we might eventually have more than four generations in one workplace in my lifetime. In other words, Gen Z is already on the way.

FOUR GENERATIONS, ONE WORKPLACE

The following section summarizes the most common characteristics of each generation, but please keep in mind that these summaries are not a perfect box that everyone will fit neatly inside. Use them simply as *clues* about where to start to better connect with and lead people of different ages. If you are born around the beginning or ending years of a generation, you will want to read what I say about "Cuspers" at the end of these descriptions.

Matures: Born pre-1946

Formative events: The Great Depression,
Pearl Harbor, World War II

Sometimes called Traditionalists or the Silent Generation, Matures' most formative experience is that they have a deeply rooted military connection. Maybe they served in the military, had friends, family, or neighbors who served in the military, or someone they loved served in the military. The military was a fixture of their coming-of-age experience, both directly (think: rationing) and indirectly (Pearl Harbor). Because of their strong military connection, Matures believe it's much more important to fit in than to stand out. They have a strong sense of duty and honor. At the same time, Matures endured the Great Depression or its immediate aftermath and became conditioned to survive on as little as possible; they are the true "waste not, want not" generation. Matures are savers who take pride in doing a good job and don't feel the need to brag. They have a strong belief in delayed gratification (which is why they have no problem driving slowly—even in the fast lane).

My grandfather is 87 years old and a proud member of the Mature generation. When I ask him to tell me about the war, all he will say is, "We left a lot of good people behind." That's it. Nothing more. He didn't keep his Army uniform or any of the photographs. Name brands mean little to him except "Cadillac," which he would never allow himself to buy, and he reuses all kinds of things that I never thought could be reused (like sandwich bags). He lives on an unbelievably small amount of money. He never offers advice unless asked. He is a good listener, extremely patient, and truly one of my heroes. My respect for him is not surprising considering that, according to my research, *Matures are the generation that Gen Y most trusts.* We find them to be highly ethical, unwaveringly loyal, and lacking the need to show off—a perfect complement to us!

Baby Boomers: Born 1946 to 1964

Formative events: Cold War, Civil Rights Movement, Vietnam, First Moon Landing

The workaholics of the modern workplace are the Baby Boomers—and for good reason. Boomers entered the workforce. They quickly realized the key to job security and career success was to outwork the competition, which they still do to this day. They arrive at work early, stay late, work on weekends and expect others to do the same (except their own kids). In other words, Boomers figured out the rules to get ahead in business, and they play to win. Boomers have only one method for measuring hard work and work ethic: hours worked per week. And the hours must be seen to count! As one Boomer manager told me, "Sure, our employees can telecommute, as long as they still show up to work in the office 40 hours a week, from 8 to 5." As bosses, Boomers believe there are no shortcuts to success at work; you must pay your dues. You cannot skip a step. Boomers are always busy, but a word of advice to Gen Y: Never ask your Boomer boss what they're busy doing. They will say, "It's complicated."

Given the Boomers' faith in work, desire to climb the company ladder, and increasing longevity in the workplace, it is no surprise they are now the most influential generation in the workplace. They are the decision-makers in most organizations. They are also my most common audience. While Boomers will not retire en masse as once feared (Thank goodness, because they know all kinds of cool things my generation doesn't, *like state capitals.*), they will eventually start to ease up on the long work hours and late nights and begin to pursue more lifestyle-friendly jobs. Ironically, Boomers will eventually start to follow the advice they gave their Gen Y kids, the same advice that is now frustrating Gen Y's employers: "Don't follow the money. Do what makes you happy."

My dad is a true Baby Boomer. He was born in 1952. He started working when he was 13 (I know because he's told me about a hundred times). He still works two jobs, and doesn't think I work hard enough (because I take breaks). My dad still carries a checkbook (How cool is that?), thinks arriving five minutes early means you're 10 minutes late, and refuses to depend on a computer. He even goes to the bank, and *actually goes inside!* When I really want to mess with him, I change the ring tone on his cell phone. He has to go over to his neighbor's house to get the Gen Yer who lives there to change it back. Awesome. Simply put, Boomers are workaholics who compete to get what they want, and when they win, they want to hear the applause.

Generation X: Born 1965 to 1976

Formative events: Watergate, PC Boom, Latchkey Kids

The generation that I feel has gotten the worst deal in our current multigenerational workforce is Generation X. They are the sandwich generation: they have been waiting and waiting and waiting to move up in their organization, yet the Boomers refuse to leave. Gen X is looking up the corporate ladder at them and thinking, "Would you retire, or at least type faster?!" And now Gen Y is on its heels going, "Mentor me, or I'll blog about you." In fact, *my interviews reveal that the most stress between generations in the workforce is not youngest to oldest, but Generation X to Gen Y.* Generation X is listening to Gen Y complain about our dissatisfaction with our rate of promotion and thinking, "Who do you think you are that you can just walk right in here and act like I owe you something? I've been waiting for my turn, and so can you."

Generation X came of age during a time of scandals, wars, fallen heroes, and government institutions that failed to deliver on promises made. They have witnessed everything from downsizing and out-sourcing to rising divorce rates and lines at the gas pump. They saw typewriters become outdated, along with job security. Major corporations broke the lifetime employer/employee promise by laying off Generation X's parents and older friends, and then offering no apology—only a rusty locked gate.

The result is that Generation X is notoriously skeptical and, I think, for good reason. Their current frustration with feeling stuck in the workforce is only adding to that skepticism. I often joke in my keynotes that Generation X double-checks my data *while* I'm speaking. They take no one at face value. Generation X is also responsible for one huge shift in employee relations. They are the first generation to enter our current workforce and think they might work somewhere else one day. This was in direct contrast to many Boomers, who entered the workforce hoping for lifetime employment, a pension, and, if they made it to the very top, a company car.

While Generation X brought a new skepticism to employer/employee loyalty, ironically they are often viewed as the most loyal generation in the workplace. However, they are loyal to *individuals*, not *organizations*. If Generation X gets a boss they believe in and trust, they will follow him or her anywhere. On the other hand, if Generation X gets a boss they don't like, they immediately start looking for a new job. That is markedly different from Boomers, who expected to have bad bosses during their career; that's why it was called "work." Since Generation X is skeptical about organizations, they've chosen to create job security by learning new workplace skills, because they believe that it is these skills that give them career options. The more career options they have, the more secure they feel about their career.

My wife is in Generation X. She is six years older than I am. We started dating, and I did exactly what a Gen Yer does: I sent her lots of important text messages. Things like: ☺; !; U. Even the famous blank "fill in your own message" text. For an entire month I sent her text messages and never got a response! I was starting to get frustrated when one day we were at lunch and her cell phone went off. She looked at the phone with annoyance and asked, "What is wrong with my phone? It has been making these noises for a month!" She didn't know what a text message was. Now *that* makes me LOL.

By the way, *you know you're over 30* if you spell out all the words in your text messages. *You're over 40* if you use commas . . .

Gen Y (aka Millennials): Born 1977 to 1995

Formative events: Baby Boomer Parents, Internet, September 11th

Gen Y, my own generation, is the fastest growing demographic in the U.S. workforce. Many of us, regardless of socioeconomics, were saved from consequences and overwhelming struggle by our well-intentioned Boomer parents. At the same time, Gen Y has been told over and over that if we can dream it, we can achieve it. (My muscles should be arriving any day now.) We are dependent on technology for staying connected to everything and everyone all the time, and we are outcome driven. We also assume we will not have Social Security, yet we continue to outspend what we earn. Gen Y does not believe we must pay our dues to get ahead—and why should we, when everyone gets a trophy just for showing up (late)? We also have *never* expected to work for one employer our entire career. We believe we are uniquely talented, and that we can bring immediate value to just about any employer. Ask us. We'll tell you. We can also get our mom to verify.

Cuspers have a place, too!

If you were born within five years of the beginning or ending year of any of the four generations listed, you may feel like you have some or all of the characteristics of the generation born before or after the one listing your birth year. The term often given to people born within this 10-year window is "Cuspers," since they were born on the cusp of two different generations. Cuspers often have characteristics of both generations surrounding their birth, but their strongest characteristics tend to be related to how they were raised.

By placing the different generations in context with Gen Y and with one another, it's much easier to spot where generations are likely to come together, fall apart, and learn from one another. It's also much easier to find the common ground that a business leader can build on to make the most of every generation's strengths and personality (and typing speed).

Y-SIZE QUESTIONS

1. Based on your birth year, which generation best fits you? Based on the characteristics I describe for each generation, which one best fits you?
2. Have you seen disconnects between the different ages or generations within your organization? If so, how?
3. Do you know the percentage of each generation in your workforce based on the birth years provided in this chapter?

CHAPTER 4

An Overview on How to *Y-Size* Your Business

(Or, How to maximize Gen Y's employment value without hiring our mom, Twittering in the bathroom, or invoking the word "Dude")

It's obvious the workforce is in the midst of rapid change. Companies large and small, new and established, are feeling the pressure to do more with less. *I believe Gen Y employees are a key part of the solution.* We are entering the workforce in record numbers; we are eager to have an impact; and we can provide an attractive cost versus benefit ratio as we continue to develop our skills. The *Y-Size* process is your road map to maximizing our workplace potential.

Sure, you might have to see our potential through the glare of our lip piercing, but we have tremendous value to offer nevertheless (especially once the swelling goes down). Until then, I challenge you to see us for what we can bring to your workplace, and not just how much we have left to learn. Whoever embraces us first will reap a cost advantage now and a strategic advantage later.

To understand how big an opportunity Gen Y can be to your career and your company, let's put a number on it.

CALCULATE YOUR COMPANY'S CURRENT INVESTMENT IN GEN Y

(The more accurate your numbers, the more accurate your answers.)

How many Gen Y employees does your company currently have? If you don't know, ask someone who does, or go ahead and guess.

Answer: _____

What is the average compensation for a Gen Y employee at your company? Again, ask if you don't know; otherwise, go ahead and guess.

Answer: _____

Now multiply the number of Gen Y employees by our average compensation.

Answer: _____

This last answer is your company's current financial investment in Gen Y as employees. You can also view this investment as the risk your company is taking by assuming that Gen Y will meet your employment needs. The better you manage this investment and decrease your risk based on my *Y-Size* process, the better the return for *everyone* involved—employers and Gen Y.

To consider your company's Gen Y employee investment in the big picture of your operations, compare us to your company's total revenues or total employee costs. To see how rapidly this reliance might grow, multiply the average compensation of a Gen Y employee by the number of us your company is likely to employ five years from today. You can reach this number by considering trends such as your five-year growth plan, average annual turnover, and percentage of new hires likely in Gen Y. The answers to these questions always lead to the same reaction from my clients: "&#*%!" Or as a Gen Yer would text, "OMG!"

Clearly, the more value your company can gain from your Gen Y employee investment—both in the present and in the near future—the more successfully your company will operate. If you understand the need (and accompanying urgency), the question to answer now is: What do you do?

MANY HAVE TRIED, BUT NO COMPANY HAS PERFECTED GEN Y EMPLOYMENT

"Okay, so, what do I do?"

That was exactly the question I was asked over and over by seasoned Fortune 500 executives, mid-level managers, and first-time entrepreneurs who wanted to know how to better employ Gen Y. To find the answer, I went in search of a company or an individual who had figured out exactly how to best employ Gen Y through our *entire* employee lifecycle (from attracting us to keeping us for years as we fill increasingly important internal job openings).

I interviewed executives, managers, entrepreneurs, corporate board members, and frontline Gen Y employees. I talked with them in-person, by phone, at their place of business, during roundtable discussions, and via e-mail in industries ranging from healthcare to fast food. I wanted to find the one person or organization that had figured out exactly how to best employ my generation. After countless conversations, e-mails, intensive research, and literally tens of thousands of airline miles, I could not find a single company or organization that was doing everything right to maximize Gen Y's employee performance from start to finish. Instead I discovered two things.

First, I found that the underlying employer / Gen Y employee issues were almost always the same. Employers wanted to attract the best and the brightest Gen Y employees, get us to show up on time (or even a few minutes early—especially if we needed to change into our uniforms), give our best effort while on the job, solve problems and innovate, develop our professional abilities, work well with others of all ages, and then stick around for more than a month (most employers said they wanted 3–5 years). This was as true in companies with 50,000 employees as it was in those with four employees sharing one cramped office, two desks, a computer, no bathroom, and a hairless dog (really).

Whether it was a hotel chain, a law firm, a tech company, or even a government entity, employers kept voicing the same concerns, albeit in their own words and occasional industry jargon. (My favorite was hearing senior partners at a huge law firm call 30-year-old associates at their firm "kids." I never felt so…10 again!) However, the level of urgency to better employ Gen Y depended entirely on our current and near-term importance to the employer's operations.

This makes obvious sense. If a company already depends heavily on Gen Y in critical positions, such as customer service in the retail industry, then management already knows the challenge Gen Y presents and wants immediate answers. Companies who are only starting to rely on Gen Y, such as those requiring more advanced degrees (which we are *finally* completing), are just beginning to realize they might have to do something different.

My second discovery was realizing how many individuals had creatively mastered one specific piece of the larger Gen Y employment puzzle. Finding these frontline-tested examples of what actually worked was the most exciting part of my journey to best employ Gen Y. One week I'd talk to a Fortune 500 executive who had found a great way to develop Gen Y talent, and another week I would listen to a small business owner who had invented a creative way to recruit quality Gen Y applicants for virtually no money. I collected these ideas with a focus on identifying those that were the most cost-effective, time efficient, and acceptable to the other generations in the workforce, and which could be customized for adoption in companies large or small. These ideas were further evaluated and refined with the help of executives, managers, and Gen Y employees themselves to determine which could work in industries as diverse as sanitation and semiconductor manufacturing, with degreed and non-degreed employees, both hourly and salaried.

THE END RESULT: A TREASURE TROVE OF STRATEGIES AND TACTICS

The end result became the foundation for this book: a treasure trove of strategies and tactics for best employing Gen Y collected from the frontlines of businesses across the board. These strategies and tactics were then refined, based on my team's additional research into Gen Y preferences, priorities, beliefs, and values. I focused on those employment aspects that executives and managers told me they most wanted help with for their Gen Y employees: accountability, retention, motivation, communication, innovation, teamwork, and overall performance.

I knew that when applied independently, the value of these strategies and tactics was positive; that's how I'd found them in the first place. But I also knew the impact was often short-term. Why? Because the actions were not connected to a larger Gen Y employment strategy. Instead, they were fragmented, with some serving as big ideas and others as extremely specific tactics. The missing link was a step-by-step framework based on the Gen Y employee lifecycle—which is much shorter than the employee lifecycle of 20 years ago—and built on an insider's understanding of Gen Y's mindset in our multigenerational workplace (i.e., someone who sleeps with his or her cell phone—yes, again, I'll admit, I'm guilty of it).

I made it my mission to develop and refine this framework until I was confident it was an *actionable methodology* that met the demands of today's challenging business climate and that also was built on the strengths of the other three generations already employed. The result is my *Y-Size* process, which begins with attracting the right Gen Y applicants and ends with keeping us longer to fill increasingly important internal job openings. The *Y-Size* process benefits Gen Y because we have a better employment experience and our talents are developed faster. The *Y-Size* process benefits you and your company because Gen Y has an impact sooner, offers greater value quicker, and will literally save you money while growing your business.

A CHAPTER-BY-CHAPTER OVERVIEW OF THE *Y-SIZE* PROCESS AND YOUR BUSINESS

Chapter 5: What Gen Y Really *Looks for in a Job*

Gen Y approaches the job search differently. To attract more high-quality applicants, you have to get us to *want* to apply as soon as we find out about your job opening (in person, online, or by phone while driving). However, receiving more applicants doesn't automatically translate into better applicants or, more important, the right applicants. This chapter will make Gen Y's approach to the job search work in your favor so that you get the right applicants applying 24/7. You will then be able to quickly weed out the applicants who don't fit while advancing the best applicants to the next step of the hiring process.

Chapter 6: Attract Quality Gen Y Employees Faster Than Free Pizza at 2 AM

In this chapter I provide four straightforward, nuts-and-bolts steps that every company—no matter the size or industry—should use to attract even more quality Gen Y applicants in a matter of days (or, if you type slowly, a matter of weeks). These ideas work. I've made them as basic as possible so that you can customize them to fit your specific situation. Each of these four ideas is cheap, and each will get your more applicants in a big way—and persuade the applicants to complete the *entire* application. I'm confident you will like the results. When you do please, let my mom know (more on that in Chapter 12).

Chapter 7: Day One Is All-Important

Gen Y decides on our first day at work whether or not we will stay with an employer long term. The unprecedented importance of the first day to Gen Y makes it the easiest opportunity you have to build a foundation for our loyalty, enthusiasm, and tenure. In this chapter I share step-by-step actions on how to make Gen Y's first day at your business so enticing that we can't wait to return—and might even show up early the next day (with roommates in tow). These ideas take only a little effort or forethought, and they consistently work. No big out-of-pocket expenses here, just ideas that will make the first day absolutely unforgettable.

Chapter 8: Orientation: Seeing Our Fit within Your Culture

Most organizations are dealing with new hires on an ongoing basis, either because of growth or turnover, and they need to standardize their orientation process for quality, consistency, and efficiency. The benefits of standardizing your orientation process are big because you see immediate payoff whether you hire two employees or 2,000. This is especially true as Gen Y represents an increasingly greater percentage of new hires. Orientation is important to us because we need to know exactly how you want us to perform. Otherwise, we have to go to you for help *all* the time, and that's a no-win for everyone (especially your e-mail inbox). In this chapter I will share several ways to make your orientation process interesting and interactive without making it more expensive. Better yet, I will add accountability to the mix so that you can hold Gen Y responsible once we start working.

Chapter 9: Keep Gen Y Engaged @ Work

My interviews with Gen Y reveal that the first 30 days of employment largely determine our career trajectory with your company for the next 30 months. The sooner Gen Y employees find our fit and path within your organization and are able to identify and measure the results most important to you, the sooner you can begin to earn a significant return on your hiring investment. You don't want Gen Y simply showing up *at* work; you want us showing up ready *to* work and keeping that focus throughout the day. Engagement is all about having us do the right things at the right time to move you and your company ahead.

Chapter 10: Develop Gen Y Talent by Making "Good Enough" Unacceptable

Gen Y has tremendous talent (just ask, we'll tell you!), but that talent is only raw potential until you draw it out of us. In this chapter I will show you where Gen Y needs the most help developing our workplace talent, and specific ways to get us to put it to use for you. By taking these actions to develop our workplace mindset and skills, you make us more valuable to you and your company from the inside out. You also prepare us to take on greater leadership roles as we build a track record of success. Your goal: transform our latent talent into action.

Chapter 11: Professionalism Is More Than Bling

Okay, so some of us Gen Yers (myself included) don't always understand what you mean by "corporate attire." We really thought our leather sandals counted. After all, the price tag said "Dress Sandals."

No worries. All the professionalism you think we need can be learned—from a good handshake to speaking in front of an audience—if you take a moment to teach us. Don't fall victim to the mistake that many managers make when they assume that Gen Y is unprofessional. It's simply that many of us lack instruction. I will show you how to accomplish this necessary instruction in 30 minutes or less, and do so only once. "OK Grasshopper, here is how you shake hands correctly. Notice how we're not hugging or bumping chests."

Chapter 12: Motivate Gen Y by NOT Giving Us a Trophy

Discretionary effort, going above and beyond the minimum required, is the sign of a motivated employee. To create discretionary effort, and to keep us motivated to produce results after we get into the groove of a new job, business leaders must build a logical and emotional connection with Gen Y employees. This type of connection doesn't cost more money. In fact, it will save you *a lot* of money and keep you from handing out all those gift cards we don't actually use (Great, a free car wash. I don't own a car.). All it takes to more effectively motivate us is an approach more in sync with our life priorities. The end goal is to make Gen Y feel so dissatisfied doing the minimum at work that doing our best is all that feels normal.

Chapter 13: Retain Gen Y—and Our Enthusiasm

To maximize the payoff from the *Y-Size* process, you want your best Gen Y employees to stay with your company for a long period of time. In this chapter, you will learn how to keep Gen Y excited about our career with your company and have us demonstrate this enthusiasm through increased average tenure. This chapter will prove that your *Y-Size* efforts are paying off because you will be able to measure your tenure results, year after year. Now *that* is Gen Y ROI!

Chapter 14: Lead Me to Loyalty

As Gen Y moves forward within an organization, we look for reasons to continue giving our best, even when the going gets tough (or, worse, the Internet slows down). The best loyalty-building connections are between us and senior leaders, as well as our colleagues. These connections can develop and evolve in both professional meetings and in less formal settings. Contrary to some expert opinions, Gen Y does not need tons of in-depth communication (i.e., keep your multi-page memo to yourself; we only read the bullet points anyway). However, we do want to know what our leaders are thinking (in 140 characters or less—preferably without vowels) and how we can help. In this chapter you will see how to make Gen Y feel included and appreciated, whether that is with a "touch-in" text message, or by making a Values Video with our boss and coworkers.

Chapter 15: Build a Talent Pipeline Like American Idol

Once you've *Y-Sized* your Gen Y employee life cycle, and your company is seeing the benefits of a new generation building momentum toward your strategic goals, it's time to lock in your advantage by developing a Talent Pipeline. Your Talent Pipeline attracts the best and the brightest *before* we start our careers so that we literally build our future with you from the ground up (and possibly before we start shaving). This is how you solidify your advantage and really peeve your competition. This is also where you start to see the ripple effects of your leadership changing your business, and at the same time changing entire lives.

WHERE TO START?

Before implementing the *Y-Size* process, it's important to figure out what's working and what's not with your current Gen Y employees. Most of my clients are able to identify at least one or two priority employment areas where they would like to focus their efforts before they spread the *Y-Size* process throughout their entire organization. For example, if you're having problems keeping Gen Y employees for more than six months, start with the Retention part of the *Y-Size* process, Chapter 13. If you're not attracting quality candidates, then start with the Attracting part of the *Y-Size* process, Chapter 5. In an ideal consulting situation, I would want you to start at the beginning of the employee life cycle and finish with the end. But since we operate in the real world and not the ideal world (meaning you already have employees and need results *now*), you should start where you see smoke: Put out the fires first and plant the trees later.

Whether you begin with Attracting Gen Y or Retaining Gen Y, you have the benefit of knowing that most of the time-consuming trial and error has been done for you. *I've found what works to make the most of Gen Y employees.* I've also found out how to implement these strategies and tactics in a way that can easily be adjusted to fit your culture, business model, and measurable objectives—all while building on the strengths of the other generations already in your workplace. While the actual implementation may vary, the under-lying problems and solutions are the same. The long-term benefit from the *Y-Size* process is a structure and system that Gen Y can rely on to move forward within your organization every day, starting at Day One.

WHO LEADS THE WAY?

When it comes to implementing the *Y-Size* Process, the right person to lead the way depends on your urgency to gain more value from your Gen Y employees. If you see Gen Y's emergence as a poten-tial strategic advantage (as I do), then your senior leadership needs to understand the problem, recognize the opportunity, and cham-pion your efforts. If, however, you are directly responsible for Gen Y employees and need better results right away, then start where you are with whatever resources and support you have. The vast majority of the tactics in the *Y-Size* process are free or inexpensive, and the more outcomes you create and document, the faster you will build support and momentum for bigger initiatives.

Regardless of where you choose to start, one thing is for certain: *The sooner you act, the more you and your company will benefit.* Gen Y is not going away; we are entering the workforce in record numbers and have the potential and desire to make a difference. Be the leader who wisely sees the opportunity and embraces our strengths and weaknesses, as well as the opportunity we represent. Lead us to the type of perform-ance and loyalty we can deliver by implementing the *Y-Size* process. We want to make an impact from Day One. Let us.

Y-SIZE QUESTIONS

1. What percentage of your workforce is in Gen Y (born between 1977 and 1995)?
2. Do you have any recruiting, training, or talent development processes especially designed for Gen Y?
3. Do you believe you could achieve better results employing Gen Y?

CHAPTER 5

What Gen Y *Really* Looks for in a Job

(Or, We only focus on money when you're not offering what we really want.)

Can you imagine quality Gen Y applicants lined up to work for you? Even better, can you imagine them lined up for the chance to *apply* to work for you? For many employers, despite the ugly economy, attracting quality Gen Y job applicants has not been as easy as they expected. However, one franchise has been able to attract quality applicants, especially Gen Y, in both good and tough economic times, just by changing up the typical recruiting process.

That company is Cold Stone Creamery, a 1,400-plus store ice cream franchise with locations in 12 countries. What is their secret to attracting quality applicants? They repositioned their initial job interview as *an audition*. That's right, an *audition* for a job. Cold Stone uses an audition format because they have found that it attracts a much larger applicant pool (especially with Gen Y, because we bring our friends!). It also distinguishes their employment opportunity from their competition (which, quite often, is located on the same street). The audition format saves management time, because it allows them to quickly determine if a potential applicant is a fit for their culture—and do so with numerous potential applicants at the same time. Finding the right cultural fit is critical at Cold Stone, because their employees are really ice cream entertainers (think: singing, telling jokes, and occasionally juggling ice cream, all while customers wait in line).

Each audition attracts between 6 and 20 people, who start the audition by giving their best three seconds of any talent or quirky trick they have—really. Examples include telling your best joke, playing air guitar, and even doing the moonwalk. Each individual then sings one of the Cold Stone tip songs as a solo. Finally, the audition group is divided into smaller groups, who have 10 minutes to write their own song and sing it—with bonus points for choreography! The individuals who do the best during the audition get a callback—just like in Hollywood—for a more traditional interview.

By simply rebranding their initial recruiting process as an audition, Cold Stone attracts more quality Gen Y applicants, saves time screening them, and stays true to their culture. Now *that's* something to sing about (and learn from)!

The Cold Stone story also provides a great introduction to the *Y-Size* process. The first step to *Y-Size* your business is to attract more quality Gen Y applicants. To me, a quality Gen Y applicant is one who has the mindset, skill set, and career potential to satisfactorily complete the tasks involved in the job you are seeking to fill. Employers tell me finding this combination is proving to be a surprising challenge, even though unemployment is at a 25-year high.

Sure, some companies are receiving an avalanche of applicants, but that doesn't mean these are automatically high-quality applicants, dependable applicants (the kind who show up without you having to drive them), or that they are the right fit for your company.

WHAT MAKES QUALITY GEN Y EMPLOYEES DIFFICULT TO ATTRACT

The difficulty companies have attracting quality Gen Y job applicants, even in an employer's market, stems from Gen Y approaching the job search differently from previous generations *and from employers being slow to adapt.* When compared with previous generations, Gen Y simply has different job search hot buttons, and these don't always mesh well with traditional hiring strategies. I believe that *Y-Sizing* presents a *stellar hiring opportunity* for companies that choose to adjust and make our approach fit their hiring outreach.

I was reminded of how different Gen Y's job search approach can be when I overheard two distinctly different Gen Y conversations at the same coffee shop. One of them was a twentysomething who was excitedly telling her friend how she had just landed a job by following an executive's Twitter feed. She posted a comment to the executive, which landed her an e-mail exchange, a job interview, and ultimately a job. I was very proud of that Gen Y job search!

On the flip side, two Gen Yers were talking at a different table near mine (while I was writing this book). One of them was a new college graduate who was complaining to her friend how hard it was to find a job "in this economy." She said she was exhausted after working *so hard* that day trying to find a job. Her friend asked how long she'd spent looking. She replied, "I used up the *entire* morning searching the Web for a job, like from 10 to 11:30." The friend replied, "Wow, you are serious about finding a job." I almost choked on my coffee.

The different extremes Gen Y brings to the job search are well known to anyone who does hiring today. Consider the following examples from actual Gen Y job applications, as told to me (without giving away names) by managers and HR directors:

1. At 4:16 AM we received a job application online. It was submitted again at 4:18 AM and 4:20 AM. (The Gen Y applicant later told us he thought this would improve his chances.)
2. When asked for two job references, the Gen Y applicant listed his mom and dad—separately.
3. Instead of writing male or female in the blank that said "Sex: _____," the applicant wrote "Yes."

Obviously, Gen Y is entering the workforce with a new approach to finding work (and some entertaining answers for fill-in-the-blank questions).

As different as the two coffee shop conversations I overheard may seem on the surface—and as extreme as the three application examples I shared may appear—*Gen Y has almost universally the same job search hot buttons.* These are the areas where you should focus your recruiting efforts in order to attract more quality Gen Y applicants. Once you learn our job search hot buttons (revealed below), you can position your company and career opportunities with *Y-Size* enticements through channels that we trust (detailed in the next chapter). You want us to be so instantly intrigued when we stumble across your employment opening that we apply for the job the moment we learn about it—even if that is at our current job or during dinner with our parents.

WHAT GEN Y LOOKS FOR IN AN EMPLOYER

Above all else, even the sought-after power to invent our own job title, Gen Y wants an employer that fits our lifestyle, personality, and priorities. Note that I didn't list money as one of the top three. I've seen time and again that while money is certainly important to Gen Y (and especially to our parents, who would love to get their spare bedroom back), we will jump to a job with lower pay if it is positioned correctly.

Gen Y's focus on lifestyle, our personal "fit within a company," and the opportunity to be challenged while advancing our career are just some of the reasons that *I believe competition to attract us has never been more level between large and small companies whose pay differential may exceed $10,000.* It also explains why nonprofits, government agencies, and other organizations that historically have been unable to compete on salary alone can now attract quality Gen Y talent—by focusing on our non-paycheck priorities. For a member of Gen Y, the deciding factor between taking a job or not taking a job often has less to do with starting salary and more to do with company culture and our initial interactions with a potential direct supervisor.

One Gen Yer said it to me like this, "I went to work for this company not because of the salary or benefits. I didn't really understand what 'benefits' were. I went to work for this company because when

I asked for information about the job, Stephanie, who is now my boss, made the job seem interesting and fun. She said, 'Let me tell you about what we do first, and if it sounds like something you would like, then I'll give you an application.' I ended up getting another job offer at the same time Stephanie offered me a job, but I chose to go with Stephanie because she made her job seem like *the perfect fit for me.* Until I went to work for her, I never imagined working in an office could be challenging and fun."

Gen Y wants to work in an environment where our bosses see us as individuals, stretch us to grow every day, and expect us to contribute immediately. (In the next chapter I will show you how to incorporate all three of these aspects into *every* job posting.) We also are hungry for a company that exhibits strong ethics and a compelling mission. All of these Gen Y desires can work to an employer's benefit, because none of these cost you more money to offer or deliver. In fact, *every one of these can save you money or make you money*, if you put them front and center in your recruiting efforts.

Once you know what Gen Y wants when looking for a job, you can adapt your existing recruiting approach and messaging (how you present the opportunity) to achieve immediate, measurable results. When you do this you make sure we find what we are looking for at your company way *before* we even apply. The big step is to adapt your recruiting efforts to match our 10 dominant job search hot buttons.

TEN HOT BUTTONS THAT INSTANTLY CONNECT WITH GEN Y JOB SEEKERS

To get Gen Y's attention faster than an IM at 4 AM, start thinking of ways to make the following 10 Gen Y hot buttons part of your recruiting strategy. (These hot buttons are relevant whether you have an entire recruiting department or *you* are the entire recruiting department.) I will share what I've seen work to bring these hot buttons to life in the next chapter.

1. Fun

Gen Y wants a fun work environment. Show us what makes your company a fun place to be. This doesn't mean it has to be all high fives or low stress; we just want to know that working at your company can be enjoyable even at the craziest time of day.

2. Challenge

Show us the types of challenges we will face in our first month and year that will test our abilities, resilience, and develop our skills. We want to conquer problems (and *then* get the trophy).

3. Creativity

Let us know how you give us the space and trust to be creative at work. This doesn't mean we need permission to dye our hair colors to match our shoelaces. It just means that we are allowed to color outside the lines—ideally on the outside of the policies and procedures manual.

4. Opportunity

We have *big* expectations for our future. Where is our path to the top with your company? Connect the dots for us and show us alternative paths to where we want to go, even if our priorities shift. Help us to see that your organizational chart is not Tetris (or, if it is, that we at least get to play with both hands and unlimited life).

5. Ethics

Your leaders stand for some level of ethics; tell us what they believe. List your company values and principles, and give specific examples of how you stuck to them in trying times. In an ideal situation, attach a media clip or firsthand testimonial for reinforcement.

6. Entrepreneurship

Let us know how you give us a sense of ownership on the job. Maybe this is achieved by allowing us to lead our own project, create a separate P&L for our position, or participate in a company-wide competition to develop a new product or service.

7. Lifestyle

This is the big enchilada of the Gen Y job search! Detail all the ways you support a Gen Y friendly lifestyle, *especially* if you can't compete on pay. This is where you emphasize flexible scheduling, nearby live music venues, outdoor activities, dodgeball teams, and free passes to cool events like Flugtag. (More on this in Chapter 14.)

8. Diversity

Gen Y is the most diverse generation in recent U.S. history. Show us how you embrace all types of diversity so that we can bring our whole self to work. The more inclusive the culture of your company, the more we feel we can be ourselves (within the dress code).

9. Technology

We love gadgets and trying out new technology. Highlight our chances to be an early adopter in your workplace by detailing how you let employees test new technology or make company information and people available to us via technology.

10. Mission

Describe the "why" behind your business and how you measure your progress toward that mission. The more tangible the progress, the better (think: candid customer testimonials). When you bring your mission to life, you offer Gen Y a chance to be part of the difference and play a role in the joyous results.

You then apply these 10 hot buttons to each of Gen Y's three primary job search channels: online, in person, and on paper. Having spent *a lot* of time researching these channels and knowing firsthand Gen Y's short attention span (try speaking to 500 of us in a room with no windows when the power goes out, including the microphone and lights), I've found specific phrases and positioning that grab our attention. I call these Gen Y's "Take Action" Job Search Cues. These are the text, sound, and imaging that get us to stop scrolling, bookmark a page as "must-visit-again," and then forward it to our parents and friends to find out what they think about the job.

GEN Y'S "TAKE ACTION" JOB SEARCH CUES

Make me feel special

More than anything else, Gen Y applicants want to be seen as unique and one-of-a-kind. Show us how a career with your company is designed specifically to fit each of us *as an individual*. Enterprise Rent-A-Car promotes on its career web site:

"Your Career. Let's Get It Started."

Make it feel personal

Make the application process all about *us* finding the right job within *your* company. The message is simple but powerful. You do this by offering us simple like/dislike questions so that we can match our interests with your job opportunities. You can also reinforce this message by using an actual HR person's name as the e-mail contact, rather than generic@ . . . Show us that we can make our career fit who we are and where we want to go, and assure us that you are human, too.

Give us some instant gratification

Gen Y gets a strong sense of satisfaction and self worth when you let us know that you noticed we applied. Your response to our application gives us the check-in and instant reassurance we crave and confirmation that we are being seriously considered. It also gives us evidence to show dad that we really are looking for a job. You might even consider giving us some sort of reward for applying, such as a discount coupon. Now you've received our application *and* encouraged us to come for an in-house visit (and buy something).

Make it entertaining

It's no secret that Gen Y is bored easily. We grew up with TVs dangling in the back of the minivan, handheld video games, YouTube, and over 100 cable channels. To make your company stand out as *the* place to work, all you need is a little dose of creativity, a digital camera or camcorder, one very hyper employee, and a contest, such as one where employees are challenged to make a homemade 60-second video explaining why people should apply to join their team. More on this in the next chapter.

Be authentic

Gen Y has a nose (sometimes studded) that can sniff out canned corporate branding a mile away. We have come of age with commercial messages bombarding us on our cell phones, computers, TVs, radios, park benches, bathrooms, and even school buses. We pride ourselves on being able to tell what is authentic and what is fluff. (In other words, stop with the employee pictures that are obviously shots of models who don't work at your company and replace them with pictures of real employees—and then tell us each employee's position at your company.) Here's an easy way to be authentic: Start an employee blog and don't fix the grammatical errors.

Simplicity rules

Long words and fancy operational diagrams do not make a job appealing or impressive to Gen Y. In fact, they make our eyes glaze over in a sweat-laced flashback to SAT prep classes. We want to be able to quickly understand what we might be doing for your company if we were hired. (And skip the part about cleaning the parking lot before each shift.) If a high school student can't explain your job opening after reading your job description, then make it simpler and add three bullet points.

When you combine Gen Y's job search hot buttons and "Take Action" Cues, you get a generation looking for employment in a whole new way—and often when the rest of the world is asleep. One retail manager said it this way:

> Gen Y is very different from my other job applicants. Gen Yers will show up at my store and kind of check out the place, and then take a job application on their way out. Then they will return later, with three friends, and they will apply *as a group*. I would never have taken my friends with me to apply for a job, let alone risk them ever meeting my potential boss, but Gen Y has a completely different way of deciding where they want to work.

TIME TO RECRUIT DIFFERENTLY

For those managers on the front lines of hiring Gen Y, it's obvious why traditional recruiting methods are seemingly less effective (and more expensive, given the ROI) than in the past. No longer can you simply place a 3x3 "Help Wanted" ad in the Sunday paper (you mean, like printed?) and expect quality applicants to call (unless you want our dads to apply on our behalf). You can't even post a generic job description on Monster.com unless you are okay with generic applicants who are racing to meet their goal of applying 100 times before Happy Hour. Instead, your job opportunity must be *Y-Sized* to attract the quality Gen Y applicants you can rely on.

In the next chapter I will provide you with detailed, inexpensive actions that take the job search insights in this chapter and apply them to our most important job search channels. Keep in mind that attracting Gen Y is all about *positioning* and *presenting* your company as a place that gets what Gen Y is about. When you do this, you put yourself and your job openings *way* ahead of the competition, especially those companies who are only now starting to use Twitter to attract Gen Y applicants. (It's like being above the fold on page 1 of a Google search.)

Y-SIZE QUESTIONS

1. Are you attracting enough quality Gen Y applicants to meet your needs?
2. How do you showcase what makes your company a special place to work?
3. What is your most effective Gen Y recruiting method?

CHAPTER 6

Attract Quality Gen Y Employees Faster than Free Pizza at 2 AM

(So you hear: "Can my friends apply, too?")

Want to know what Zappos employees are thinking right now? If you're a Gen Y job seeker, you sure do. Luckily for us, we can go to http://twitter.zappos.com/employee_tweets and see what their employees are thinking and doing right this second.

Really.

I'm sure the very thought of this much transparency strikes fear into the hearts of many executives—especially those who covet their company's privacy. Don't worry, I'm not asking you to start tweeting about your company's trade secrets, but I will ask you to think about the image your company is projecting to potential applicants—especially the high-value ones you most want.

There are four *Y-Size* steps that will immediately help your company attract and hire more quality Gen Y employees (meaning the kind you *want* to hire). The steps outlined in this chapter address the sometimes radically different needs of Gen Y (such as completing applications without having to borrow a pen) and also fit the reality of what today's employers can offer on a tight budget. You can apply each of these four steps individually, but for best results try to use at least some variation of them all. This consistency across your employment messaging maximizes your results, whether Gen Y finds you online, in line, or hears about you from a friend (which is critical, because our friends are our most trusted job referral source).

STEP 1: MAKE YOUR WEB SITE A GEN Y EMPLOYMENT EXPERIENCE

From Gen Y's point of view, *your company's career web site is your company's job opportunity.* I know this because almost every Gen Y employee I've ever interviewed said they went to a potential employer's web site *before* deciding whether or not to apply for a job and definitely before deciding whether or not to accept a job offer. (We also forwarded the site to our friends for their opinion before we made our decision.) This makes your web site central to your recruiting efforts. It is why I always begin my process of helping companies attract more quality Gen Y applicants by first *Y-Sizing* their web site.

If your web site appears old (think 1990s clip art), out of touch (i.e., dated ancient, like 2005), and nothing moves (including your hosting connection), then it's reasonable for Gen Y to assume that working at your company feels the same way. At the same time, updating a company web site to connect with Gen Y job seekers is cheap. It also leads to immediate, *measurable* results. You don't have to create your own avatar or load up each page with Web 2.0 features (although you can, if you have the budget); all you have to do is simply address Gen Y's 10 job search hot buttons the moment we load your career page—and it should only take a moment. If that takes longer than five seconds, we've already moved on to your competitor's page.

The following section provides crucial actions you can take to *Y-Size* your web site so that you attract more Gen Y applicants right away:

- *Remove all photos in the employment area of your web site that were not taken at your company*, unless they feature your customers or some other company-related event, mission, or project. Replace these stock photos (e.g., the obviously posed cheesy ones where the lighting is just right) with pictures of actual employees doing their jobs and having fun. For examples of this *Y-Size* technique, check out www.ysize.com/ch6.
- *Video Gen Y employees talking candidly about what they do at their job on a regular day.* Ask them to mention any particularly interesting projects they've recently completed or challenges they had to work to overcome. The key is to *not* film these in a professional studio but on site, preferably in an employee's cubicle or work area. The secret is to post these videos on your company's site and, more importantly, on YouTube. Why? Because the YouTube video is more likely to be forwarded. You can even have the YouTube video appear directly on your site for free. If you really want to make this memorable, organize a contest where you ask your employees and/or managers to create and film a 60-second commercial on why the viewer should apply to be on their team. The more hyper and unexpected, the better. For examples of employees talking about their employer, check out www.ysize.com/ch6.
- *Set up a recruiting group or young professional employee group on popular social networking sites such as Facebook, Twitter, or Linkedin.* Promote this online group as a place where potential Gen Y applicants can connect with current employees around our own age as well as meet recruiters to get our questions answered and get exposure to some elements of your company's culture. Try to use social networks where dialogue is encouraged and where you can also send private replies. Don't make this group overtly self-promotional; instead, position yourself and the group as a 24/7 free career resource. For examples of this taken from actual company web sites, check out www.ysize.com/ch6.
- *Create a simple and entertaining introduction to your company.* You can make it a slideshow with a narrator voiceover or, if you're a big company, show a history of your commercials. Either way, include several lists, such as "Five Things You Probably Don't Know

About Our Company" (the quirkier the better) or "Ten True or False Questions About Our Company and Industry." For links to these types of introductions, including one with a welcoming avatar, visit www.ysize.com/ch6.

- *Post and validate your company's ethics, values, and mission online.* Gen Y is hugely attracted to ethics. Companies should prominently list their core values and ethics on their employment page and, if possible, their homepage. Even better, post videos or photos of your employees putting these ethics into action. For examples of this taken from actual company web sites, check out www. ysize.com/ch6.

- *Offer a virtual tour of your company or a virtual Day One.* Remember that Gen Y often decides on our very first day at work if we will stay with a company long-term. One solution: Post a video that follows a day in the life of a new hire and another one that follows someone with three years' experience. Be sure to show everything, from where we work and eat to what we really do. Virtual tours taken from actual company web sites can be found at www. ysize.com/ch6.

- *Clearly explain how your company focuses on achieving growth by developing its people.* Mention all types of training programs, orientation courses, and leadership development pathways for new hires and young professionals. An effective way to showcase these is to spotlight a few younger employees who have swiftly advanced within your company. You can see examples of this on actual company web sites at www.ysize.com/ch6.

- *Start an employee blog.* On this blog, let employees share what they are doing and learning. This generates lots of new content for your web site, which can help with search engine optimization (meaning better search ranking results) and gives your site an authentic feel. For examples of employee blogs taken from actual company web sites, including Microsoft, which offers a menu of employee blogs on their web site, check out www.ysize.com/ch6.

- *Match potential applicants with your current job openings.* You can do this by asking us to input our interests, strengths, education, experience, and so on, and then have our answers automatically match with jobs you currently have open. Or, you can simply give us the option to browse your openings based on certain requirements,

such as minimum degree. To make this matching even more powerful, you can follow the lead of Southwest Airlines, which offers
job seekers who visit their career web site the option to receive an
e-mail when a position opens that fits their specified criteria. For
links to company web sites that allow you to find opportunities
based on your interests, visit www.ysize/ch6.

If you want more ways to make your web site attractive to Gen Y,
ask your current Gen Y employees for their top five suggestions.
Then ask them to ask a few friends for their suggestions and for
examples of other company employment web sites they think are
cool. Some of their ideas will be insightful, and others (like streaming
the NCAA tournament on your company site), yeah, not so much.

The real beauty of using the Web to attract more and better applicants is that you don't have to be a big company with deep
pockets to get great results. You also get the immediacy of being
able to see your changes right away and measure the results, thanks
to applications such as Crazy Egg and Google Analytics. If you
don't know about these types of applications, check them out at
www.crazyegg.com and http://www.google.com/analytics/.

After you've *Y-Sized* your web site, you've got to get the word
out *everywhere*. Here's how:

- *Print your career URL on everything.* And I mean everything. If
  you're a tech company, promote your career URL to customers
  who download an advanced version of your technology. If you're
  a quick-service restaurant, put it on napkins, receipts, and table
  displays. If you're a shipping company, let us know you're hiring
  when we track our package. Your current Gen Y customers can
  become your best Gen Y employees. They already like your brand.
- *Offer free stuff to visit your career web site.* These incentives don't have
  to be financial. They can be a free ringtone download, a coupon
  for your goods or services, bonus points for your frequent shopper
  club, or a behind-the-scenes video that shows how your products
  go from idea to store shelves.
- *Launch a contest that people enter via your career web site.* For example, if your organization is an education company, ask us how we
  would improve a school for under $50. Or if you work for a bank,

ask us how we would get more young people to save money in 100 words or less. Give the winner something fun, and automatically ask participants if they want to apply for a job.

- *Sign up to have a phone number where potential applicants can send a text message and automatically receive a link to your online application.* This is inexpensive to set up, easy to promote, and it shows that you embrace new technology, which Gen Y loves. (It also keeps us from losing your paper application on the way home.)

Hint: Test drive your current career web site on your cell phone. If it's hard to navigate, consider offering a mobile-friendly version. And if you just read this and thought, "I can't surf the Web on my phone," then, my friend, it's time to get a new phone.

Once Gen Y applies online, automatically send us a short e-mail outlining the next steps in your hiring process. Ask us if we would like to receive your e-newsletter or be notified of recruiting or hiring events in your area. Keep us interested by sending short tidbits of information every week or two. You can even send us recommended reading or suggested resources that will help us prepare for the application process (which you can later reference to determine how motivated we are to land the job). By staying in touch virtually, you keep us interested, and, as an added bonus, you separate yourself from the rest of the companies from which we never heard from again and don't know why.

STEP 2: GIVE APPLICANTS SOMETHING OFF THE PAGE ON THE JOB APPLICATION

While reaching Gen Y online is often the most cost-effective way to increase our job applications, many companies still rely heavily on more traditional applications. This might be based on the nature of their business, especially in the service industry, or the demographic they seek to employ (such as those with limited computer skills, Web access, or language barriers). Either way, with a little creativity you can make a traditional application—and corresponding online application—marketing tools by themselves. No YouTube video necessary, just a little ingenuity on how to make your application unexpected and in line with Gen Y's job search hot buttons.

One example of how a company merged their paper application with Gen Y's preferences is the Rudy's BBQ franchises, operated by K&N Management, Inc. These restaurants are at the top of sales for their franchise and legendary around my hometown of Austin because of the "Welcome to Rudy's!" greeting you get when you open the door. K&N uses a process called Topgrading® to hire everyone from cashiers to cooks and managers. K&N now has over 450 employees and, most impressive for their industry, annual turnover of only 50 to 80 percent. That is *less than half* of what traditional quick-service restaurants experience. Even with such low turnover for the industry, Ken Schiller, the co-owner of K&N, believes their company's success is absolutely dependent on the people staffing their restaurants. They want every Gen Yer who even thinks about applying for a job to be able to act on that instinct immediately—and without a pen.

To figure out how to get more Gen Yers to apply, K&N's management team observed how and when Gen Y applied for jobs. They wanted to see if they could find any trends. What they noticed was that many applicants applied during the lunch hour, which happens to be each location's busiest time. The applicants literally ordered Rudy's famous brisket along with a job application. Soon the applicants would be hunched over a table scribbling on their application while customers were eating next to them (everyone shares tables).

The entire process looked inefficient to the Rudy's leadership—not to mention a little strange to the customers trying to eat. So, Rudy's decided to change it. Their solution: a number dispenser next to the front door. This number dispenser is similar to one you would see in a busy meat market, but written on these tickets are instructions on how to apply for a job at Rudy's by phone or online.

Now when you ask for a job application at a K&N-managed restaurant, the person behind the counter smiles and says, "Great. We'd love to have you apply and possibly join our team. All you need to do is take a ticket from the dispenser next to the door and either call the toll-free number or apply online. Either way, you can apply 24 hours a day, seven days a week." And when an applicant calls the 800 number, the operator makes sure all the application questions are answered; the answers are documented by the person asking the questions; and the answers are then screened against Rudy's hiring priorities before anyone at the company even sees the application. Here's the best part for Gen Y: We can now apply without having to borrow a pen; we know the application is completed correctly; and we can eat our lunch without worrying about dripping that tasty BBQ sauce on our application! Brilliant.

If a number dispenser doesn't fit your company's culture or business model, maybe you can distribute a memory stick (aka thumb drive) that has a welcome greeting from an executive, tells us all about your company, and includes an employment application. Compared to the value of landing one good employee, the return is overwhelming. The lesson: Getting more Gen Yers to apply for work at your company doesn't have to take a lot of extra time or money. All it takes is a little observation and creativity. Look at *how* and *when* Gen Y applies to work for you and you will uncover opportunities to be more effective.

And now to *Y-Size* the actual application . . .

If you have to stick to a paper application or, like many companies, you prefer online applications, you can make your opportunity jump off the page by adding unexpected questions based on your company's *core values*. These questions emphasize the importance of your core values to your selection process, make your application entertaining to complete, and give you deeper insight into the applicant's thinking. Here are some nontraditional core values questions you might consider adding to your existing application:

- One of our core values is *Dependability*. If you were driving to work and your car broke down, what would you do?
- One of our core values is *Always Add Value*. If the store manager gave you the ability to change something inside the store to increase sales, what would you change?
- One of our core values is *Creativity*. Can you please make something creative with this paper bag? Note: *they actually do this as part of the application process at Amy's Ice Cream!*
- One of our core values is *Service*. What is an example of a time you sacrificed in order to help someone else?

Your current Gen Y employees are a good source for creating more of these nontraditional values-based questions, but always double-check that your questions meet state and federal hiring guidelines.

STEP 3: PROVIDE GEN Y THE ANSWERS FOR YOUR INTERVIEWS UP FRONT

At most companies, the deciding step in the hiring process is an interview or series of interviews. This presents a new challenge for employers when it comes to Gen Y, because interviewing is Gen Y's weakest real-world skill. The reason is that we often have not mastered the art of interpersonal skills (after all, some of us text our boyfriend or girlfriend while we're sitting next to them *in the car*). This inability to put our best foot forward during an interview makes it increasingly difficult for an employer to decide between a bad hire and a good hire who simply doesn't know how to interview.

How do you shake up your interview so you can tell if a Gen Yer could be a potentially great hire or a can't-wait-to-fire? Chuck Hendrix, the former president of one of the largest Gen Y employers in Texas, came up with a solution that I've seen work consistently. It all started with one untucked shirt . . .

As president of a company dependent on young staff in order to operate, Chuck always wanted to know what the applicant flow was like, so he would head down to his HR department and get a sense of what was happening at the front of the hiring process. From time to time he would even conduct interviews himself. One day he ended up interviewing an older teenager. The teen was late to the interview and slouched in his chair; his shirt was untucked; and he looked like he had just rolled out of bed. Chuck said, "You know, I can tell you right now, you're not going to get this job."

The young man was startled and offended. "What do you mean?" he asked. "You haven't even asked me any questions!"

"Look, I'll be really honest with you. You arrived late. You didn't bother to tuck in your shirt or comb your hair, and you're chewing gum," he continued. "All of this gives me the impression that you don't care whether I hire you or not. Do you really want this job?"

The young man responded with a bit of a chip on his shoulder. "Of course I want the job," he said. "I took two busses to get here. Why else would I be here?"

Chuck said, "Okay. If that's the case, here's what I'm going to do. I'm going to tell you the five most important things you need to do when you come in here for an interview so that you get the job.

And if you come back tomorrow and you do those five things, I promise that I will hire you. Here is my card. Call my executive assistant to schedule an interview and prove to me how much you want the job."

The young man left with his instructions, and—much to Chuck's surprise—he returned the next day and did everything he was told to do the day before. He brought in a completed application. He tucked in his shirt. He shook hands and looked Chuck in the eye during the interview, which was now taking place in the president's office. He sat up straight, and he left his gum in the trash. Chuck was as good as his word, and, as promised, he hired the young man on the spot—a young man who ended up becoming a great employee.

From that moment on, Chuck ran with the idea that potential applicants should be told what they need to do to get the job *before* they had an interview. Using this approach, Chuck was able to effectively screen applicants before they showed up *and* earn the respect of those he eventually hired.

He explained it to me this way:

> When you create clear expectations and let potential applicants know your expectations up-front, you've just saved yourself a tremendous amount of time—and in business, *time is money.* You're also helping to keep the entire hiring process from getting bogged down with people who aren't the right fit.

> The interview process shouldn't be about "gotcha" moments. The process should be about finding those employees who enhance your professional environment and profitability. The individual who feels uncomfortable in business attire might not be a fit for the front of the house, but could turn out to be just what you were looking for in another role.

> In a best-case scenario, you want applicants to decide before they apply whether or not they can meet your expectations. This respects your company and its resources as well as the applicant.

Simply stated, if you give an applicant clear expectations up front about what you're looking for and they choose not to apply, then you've saved yourself and them time and money. In addition, if they still apply and don't meet the expectations during the interview, then you know right away they're not a fit for your company.

I believe Chuck is on to something *big* that companies can learn from and implement. So many Gen Yers I meet have never been taught how to interview, so why not take 30 seconds to give us a few instructions on how to *earn* the job? You're not babying us; you're testing us to assess our true capabilities and motivation. If we act on your instructions, you know we are serious. If we don't, you've saved yourself a lot of time and aggravation. The easiest way to share these instructions is to put together a list of five or 10 things that applicants should do before, during, and after the interview to increase our chances of getting hired. Then print these tips right on the back of the paper application. Yes, you read that right: *Stick 'em directly on the backside of the application for every applicant to see before we apply.* Now you've added a valuable screening tool to your application process, as well as helped the applicants with talent to put our best foot forward (rather than put our Birkenstock in our mouth).

Before you think this type of baseline instruction is reserved for low-paying or low-skill jobs, you should know that many of the most prestigious companies in the United States are now providing applicants with instructions on how to interview.

McKinsey & Co. is one the most respected management consulting firms in the world and one of the most prestigious places for extremely talented young professionals to launch their careers. You don't think the brainiacs they hire directly from the best business schools need help applying? Think again. McKinsey & Co. went so far as to post a video on their web site detailing how to do well in their interview: http://www.mckinsey.com/careers/how_do_i_apply/how_to_do_well_in_the_interview.aspx.

I know you may be thinking, "Aren't we coddling these young people by telling them how to complete an application or participate in an interview? Shouldn't they be responsible for knowing what to do in the real world?" I know where these questions are coming from, especially if you yourself started on the ground floor and worked overtime for years to get where you are today. (I actually started as a busboy at Macaroni Grill, where I was taught, coincidentally, how to tie a tie. More about that later.)

While I understand the viewpoint of those critical about helping Gen Y (especially before we're even hired), my perspective as a business owner tells me that this is actually a *great opportunity* for finding unpolished talent rather than something to lament as generational ignorance. When you get right down to it, the untucked shirt is far from a foolproof litmus test for detecting the best and brightest young people. In fact, the young person may have gone to great lengths to borrow or buy that shirt; they just didn't know how to wear it correctly.

My thought is that if you and your company are missing out on potentially loyal and hardworking new hires because no one has taught us how to shake hands, look you in the eye, or dress for an interview, then why not be the one who shows us how? Then you can find the undervalued diamond in the rough sitting in front of you that others have missed (because the diamond has a poorly placed tattoo).

If you have to remind a Gen Y applicant to do something three times, then yes, it is coddling, and you absolutely shouldn't hire us (although our moms will likely call you to disagree). But if you tell us once and we act on it, and go on to the next thing, then you're not coddling us, *you're developing our skills and assessing our motivation.* You're also increasing our value as employees, which is exactly what great employers do. When you see a Gen Yer's potential rather than our, shall we say, "unique" haircut, you also lay the foundation for an emotional connection that can develop into the long-term loyalty that money alone cannot buy. All it takes is sharing some simple instructions you learned along the way, possibly from an employer who saw past your own youth and into your potential.

You can also make your interview more effective by not asking the same 10 interview questions that every other company seems to ask. I consider Jonathan Davis, CEO of American Workforce, one of the best interviewers in the country (and he has lots of well-known clients to prove it). He's always told me, "Jason, there are two hiring reasons why someone doesn't work out:

1. You personally weren't clear about what *you* needed in the role (and as a result, you hired the wrong person); or
2. You failed to clearly *tell* the new person what it was that you needed them to do *before* you hired them."

Jonathan has also been kind enough to share some of his favorite interview questions that he uses to effectively screen Gen Y candidates:

- When was the last time you used your own judgment to make a decision at work and it worked out really well?
- What about a time when it didn't work out so well?
- What did you learn from the experience when things didn't work out that you would do differently next time?
- *Then, if you're really feeling like the person you're interviewing has the maturity to handle it, one of my favorite follow-up questions is,* "How would I know that?"
- Who do you look up to and admire in your personal life?
- What are the characteristics that they exhibit that you most respect? *Thank them for sharing and then ask:*
- And do you respect those because you share the same, or because you lack them?
  Here's where it gets powerful:
- What have you done in the past 30 days to enhance your proficiency in those specific areas you've mentioned?
- Can you give me an example of how you would want to be told when you've done something exceptional at work?
- How does that compare to how you'd like me to give you feedback around something that you need to improve?
- What's the longest you've ever done any one activity for in the past (whether it's playing soccer, being in Boy Scouts, leading a Community Youth Group)? What was it about that activity that made you stick with it for so long?
- Looking back at your life to this point, what are you most proud of? Why is that?

STEP 4: OFFER GEN Y MORE THAN MONEY AND WE WILL ACCEPT LESS

It's time to seal the deal. You've found a Gen Y applicant you want to hire, and you're itching for us to start work. All that matters now is the offer. You tell us how much you're going to pay and when we can start, and we sign on the dotted line. Simple, right?

Wrong. Not so simple any more—not if you want us to accept your first offer with great enthusiasm (and brag about it on Facebook). This is especially true if you are trying to hire top-tier candidates. These candidates are likely to have multiple offers in good and challenging economic times.

To make your job offer too good to pass up, include these *Y-Size* elements:

- *Present a printed and signed official letter formally offering us the job.* Verbal or via e-mail is not enough. Putting the offer on your letterhead makes the position tangible and gives us something we can physically show our parents and friends. However, preface the letter's arrival with a phone call letting us know you're excited to extend us the opportunity join your team. If you really want to hit it out of the park, send the offer letter via overnight mail. When someone pays 15 bucks to mail us something, we feel important (and keep the envelope to prove it).

- *Explain your compensation package in simple terms.* This should include any potential bonuses, retirement options, travel reimbursements, relocation packages, and anything else that has to do with Gen Y and our paycheck. Explain everything in the simplest language possible, and consider providing URLs to web sites with more detailed definitions. If the position is largely commission-based, give us examples of what we can likely earn based on the effort we put forth.

- *List three potential career paths for us at your company, starting from our first day at work.* If you're in the software business, show us how we can go from junior programmer to senior programmer to assistant team leader, team leader, project leader, and so on. Give us a dotted line we can follow to the big payoff. The same goes for working at large companies. Show us how we can transfer from one division to another, or one location to another, as we move forward.

- *Detail a few specific projects we are likely to complete or challenges we are likely to face during our first year on the job.* Even a few examples will add excitement to your job offer.

- *Specify the talent development opportunities within your company that are open to us.* This could range from professional certifications, soft skills training, mentoring, and industry association membership to tuition reimbursement or participation in a formal Leadership Development Program.

- *Highlight your efforts to help us maintain work/life balance.* You can do this by offering flexible scheduling or telecommuting after a certain tenure period, reimbursing us for health club or wellness memberships, or sponsoring volunteer activities. You should also list any nontraditional events you organize or support, such as a company volleyball tournament or disco bowling.
- *Provide us with a list of our top accountabilities for the job.* Both you and the new hire should agree on this list up front so that you each know what to expect during an evaluation.

The more you can fine-tune your offer to include what you've learned about the *individual* Gen Y applicant, the more we will feel your company is exactly the right place for us. If you really want to guarantee we accept the offer, emphasize two or three ways you believe your company can help us reach a personal goal in the coming year. For example, if a new employee is a distance runner, you can offer for her to start and stay at work an hour late twice a week, so that she can complete her long runs and get some sleep. Any way you can show us that you're embracing each of us as individuals will make your job offer feel one-of-a-kind, which means we won't pass it up (even if it's for a little less money than someone else is offering!).

Y-SIZE QUESTIONS

1. What steps have you taken to make your web site a Gen Y employment experience?
2. How does your job application differ from your competitors' applications?
3. Do you inform potential applicants of your company's expectations before they apply?

CHAPTER 7

Day One Is All-Important

(Or, "The job sounded great, until I showed up and they didn't know who I was.")

The first day at a new job has never been as make-or-break to any generation as it is to Gen Y. The reason: Many Gen Yers decide *on our first day at work* whether or not we will stay with an employer long term. Our very first day! From my experience, I'd argue that many of us know by lunch. If by lunch we feel an employer fits our personality and future, then we'll text all our friends (and room-mates) to apply right away.

However, the opposite is also true. If our first day begins with a series of uncomfortable moments (such as you not knowing we were supposed to start today), awkward exchanges ("But no one told me I couldn't wear a halter top."), and a clear message that we are an imposition ("Look, kid, you figure it out. That's what I had to do."), we will spend the afternoon surfing the Web for a new job while tweeting about our disappointment.

THREE REASONS WHY THE FIRST DAY IS CRITICAL TO GEN Y

It is my observation that the first day at work is critically important to Gen Y for three reasons:

1. Many of us have been told over and over how successful we will be in the real world, and our first day at work is the maiden voyage of that journey. This is why our moms text us three times to see how it's going *and to confirm that we showed up.*
2. We often don't have significant workplace experience at a young age, so our expectations about work have yet to be challenged. This makes the first day at your company either validation of six long years in college (and $40,000-plus in debt) or the day our reality check bounces.
3. We decide quickly whether we like almost anything—food, relationships, even clothes we've already bought (which we've been known to subsequently return *on the same day*). Employment is no different, except it involves us waking up earlier and sharing a confined space with people who don't dress, talk, or bathe like us (for better or worse).

Here's the hidden *Y-Size* opportunity: Make the first day unforgettable and you gain our enthusiasm, *plus the interest of all our friends.* The best part is that what Gen Y wants in order to have an unforgettable first day at work is usually free, simple to do, and likely less stressful than what you're already doing—and it can reinforce to your employees of all ages what makes your company great.

The added bonus: Gen Y wants to have an impact in your organization from Day One. Let us! In this economy, you need immediate results from your hiring investment, and that's exactly what Gen Y wants to deliver. The sooner you give us permission to make a difference in your organization, the sooner we'll prove that you've made a wise hiring decision.

INGREDIENTS TO *Y-SIZE* OUR FIRST DAY

I've spent a lot of time studying and consulting on what works and what doesn't in designing a first day that Gen Y loves *and* one that gets us off to a solid start. This experience has taught me that a great first day delivers three outcomes:

- The new hire feels genuinely welcomed by our colleagues;
- The new hire gains an introduction to the company's culture and our role within the larger organization; and
- A new hire makes a connection with at least one leader in the organization.

The balancing act for most business leaders is trying to figure out how to achieve these three outcomes while running a business. After all, you're busy, the economy is challenging, and you've got other employees to worry about. You don't have time to take your eye off the ball. You also have to take into consideration your company's culture, management philosophy, current staff, and business realities.

To make this easy for you, I've constructed an ideal *Y-Sized* First Day. You can choose for yourself which elements fit your company culture and employment situation. You can also use these strategies and tactics as the basis for creating or customizing your own first day rituals. Either way, know that the first day is your absolute best chance to connect with Gen Y in a way that makes us stop looking for our next job and start working toward our first promotion.

Dan Rozycki, president of Transtec, knows the importance of a new hire's first day, especially at his engineering firm, where every employee needs to make an impact immediately. He noticed that a new hire, Sabrina, had listed her mom as a reference. This might be shocking to some people, but it's not uncommon to Gen Y—especially if we don't have a lengthy job history. Who else are we going to use as a reference, our pediatrician? Dan decided to make Sabrina's first day unforgettable (for her and the entire office) by inviting Sabrina's mom to welcome her daughter to her first day at work at her first "real job." As you can imagine, it took some convincing ("Is this a *real* business, Mr. Rozycki?"), but Sabrina's mom finally agreed.

On Sabrina's first day, the engineering firm gathered in the company's reception area to welcome her. They always welcome a new employee with a five-minute meet and greet. Sabrina's mom was waiting in the company's hallway around the corner from the reception area when Sabrina arrived. After a few minutes, Sabrina's mom walked into the reception area and completely surprised her daughter. While Sabrina was speechless, her mom was not. She turned to everyone and said, "I took my daughter to kindergarten. I took my daughter to college. And now I'm here on the first day of her career. Thank you."

Can you imagine? Afterward Dan gave Sabrina *and her mom* a tour of the company and explained to Sabrina's mom exactly why Sabrina's job was so important. On the way out Sabrina's mom told her daughter, "You're not allowed to quit this job. Real companies are not likethis." Yes!

NO NEW HIRE MONDAYS

Day One, Rule 1: Never start a new hire on Monday. Ever. This is usually the worst possible day for a person to get introduced to your company. So many problems happen over the weekend, or were put off until Monday morning, that they are now all-out crises demanding your full attention. Rather than welcome new employees by dropping us into this type of tension, start your new hires around 10 AM on a different day that works better with your business cycle. This gives you the ability to get your most pressing responsibilities out of the way on the morning a new Gen Y employee starts yet still have enough time to make the new hire feel welcome before we leave for lunch or you offer to take us. My suggestion: Take the new hire to lunch or arrange for a coworker to take them, Dutch treat, of course. Few things are less welcoming than meeting your 10 new coworkers and then having to eat alone while they talk together at a different table.

SEND A PRE-FIRST DAY E-MAIL
TO THE NEW HIRE

If possible, the day before the new hire arrives, send us an e-mail that conveys some basic company expectations and answers common but important new hire questions. These include where to park (not in the space marked CEO), who to ask for when we arrive at the workplace (again, not the CEO), appropriate dress, and anything we specifically should or should not bring. For example, some companies don't want us to bring a phone that can take pictures. (I know, because at a nuclear power plant where I was speaking, a very strong security guard confiscated my Blackberry, and I went through extreme withdrawal for the entire two hours we were apart.)

Avoid the separation anxiety generated by detaching a Gen Yer from his or her cell phone. Alert us ahead of time if things like camera phones (and open-toed shoes) are not allowed. This e-mail also gives you one more opportunity to share your enthusiasm for us joining your team—and to remind us of the time when we should arrive.

OUR UNOFFICIAL TOUR GUIDE

When the new hire arrives, make sure someone is assigned to greet us and show us around. For the time being, this unofficial tour guide represents your entire company, so pick someone who represents your company well (or at least not the employee who started the day before). This could be a coworker or boss, but I've found it is most beneficial to have someone around the new hire's age introduce us to our new workplace. Being welcomed by a peer is more comfortable for employees of all ages, but especially for Gen Y. It also creates a natural dialogue in which the new hire's questions will be answered from a similar life place (such as, Where do people hang out after work? Are there cool apartments to live in nearby? Are jeans *only* allowed on Fridays?).

SHOW US YOU MEAN BUSINESS—AND PRESENT THE CARD TO PROVE IT

The best *Y-Size* tactic I know to make the first day exceptional costs less than $20 for most employers. When a new Gen Y employee shows up for our first day, feeling all nervous and excited, greet us with a smile and a handshake. Then, present us with a small box and ask us to open it up. Inside the box are our preprinted business cards with our name spelled correctly. This unexpected gift gives you the perfect setup to say, "Welcome to the team. We're glad you're here. You now represent us, just as we now represent you. I'd like to share with you some of our expectations (say all those things you've been wanting to say). What are some of yours?" Who is the first person we are going to give our new business card to? *Our mom!* And many of us are going to give it to her right when she picks us up.

Just to prove I'm not kidding, a Baby Boomer audience member at an applied science company came up to me after a speech and was shaking his head and laughing. He told me that earlier in the day he had received an overnight mail envelope from his Gen Y son, who just started his first real job. The envelope contained 10 of his son's new business cards and a Post-It note with instructions to keep one card and give the rest to relatives!

OTHER WAYS TO WELCOME GEN Y ON OUR FIRST DAY

If a business card is too difficult to print for a new hire's first day, consider some tangible display of your enthusiasm for us joining your team. This can be as basic as a funky welcome card signed by current employees, or as Gen Y savvy as an invite to join your company's *Facebook* group the moment we accept your job offer.

One of my favorite technology companies, MyEdu.com, gives all new hires a potted plant on their first day at work. They then take a picture of the new hire holding his or her plant. This photo is taped to the outside of the new hire's cubicle or office, along with a notation listing the new hire's name and start date. The idea is that, like the plant, the new hire is going to "grow with the company."

Chris Chilek, co-founder of MyEdu, says, "I knew it sounded cheesy when I first suggested that we give each new employee a plant, but the gesture is pretty unforgettable, and Gen Y really seems to like it. At the same time, our company has been doubling in size every quarter, and we wanted some tradition that helped maintain our culture. Now when a new hire sees a senior employee's plant and how large it has grown in comparison to the picture on their door, they realize they are a part of something special. The size of the plants also show that even though we're a fast-growth company, we offer stability, which is a big plus in today's job market. The plants are now so popular that many people have started naming them!"

One very large software company where I spoke understands the importance of the first day and the need to mesh it with Gen Y's lifestyle priorities. Their HR director told me they try to start all new hires on Fridays. Why? Because at 5 PM on Fridays they serve beer at their corporate campus. Yep. Beer. They've found that an on-site Happy Hour is a good social setting for a new hire to hang out with coworkers and mingle with people from different departments. I know I'd want to go back on Monday. Heck, some of my Gen Y friends would probably stay there all weekend.

SMALL ACTS OF INCLUSION SHOW US WE BELONG

If you can't take such a big action on a new hire's first day (or serving beer is completely out of the question in the hospital where you work), remember that small acts of inclusion go a long way to show Gen Y that we've made a good decision by joining your company. One idea you might consider is to ask the new hire's primary coworkers to wear nametags through lunch. This reduces those awkward moments where everyone knows our name, but we don't know anyone else's name. It also helps us learn our coworkers' names faster, which helps us feel like part of the group faster. On the same note, *please* don't ask a Gen Y new hire to give an impromptu introductory speech to our coworkers on our first day. Public speaking is most people's greatest fear, and for many in Gen Y it's completely unnatural.

After the new hire is welcomed individually or by coworkers, it's time to introduce us to your culture by giving us the lay of the land. The best way I've seen to do this is with a walking tour of the business. The best tours walk a Gen Yer through the operational cycle. This way the Gen Yer understands how all the moving parts in your business work together, as well as our personal role within the moving parts.

BRING YOUR COMPANY'S CULTURE TO LIFE

With a proper introduction to our workspace complete, it's time to make your company's culture come alive. Start this process by walking the new hire through your Heritage Hallways (described in Chapter 14) or by having us watch your *Why We Love This Place* video, which shows your employees talking candidly about why they love their job (also explained in Chapter 14). The more homemade the video, the more credible it will appear to a new Gen Y hire. If possible, the tour guide should also talk about the company's near-term focus, long-term goals, and overall mission. Remember, your culture doesn't have to be all bells and whistles to excite Gen Y; what we connect with is authenticity and sincerity. We want to see people doing their jobs and enjoying what they do.

After you've welcomed Gen Y to your company and lifted the curtains back a bit on your culture, *only then* should you give us the required but mundane first-day mountain of paperwork that would make any old-growth forest quiver (unless you handle confidential information, in which case it's necessary for a new hire to sign a NDA or similar document before we start our first day).

END THE FIRST DAY ON A HIGH NOTE (AND I'M NOT TALKING JONAS BROTHERS)

As a capstone to the first day, find a way to introduce the new hire to at least one executive or senior leader within your organization. Even a one-minute exchange in the hallway, cafeteria, or executive's office will do. All the new hire needs to experience is shaking the executive's hand and the executive, in turn, congratulating the new hire on making a good career decision (it's even better if they know our name!). If that's too much, have an executive call us at a specific time—or, if nothing else, send an e-mail—on our first day to wish us luck and tell us why they believe so strongly in the company's future. A great first day always ends with a positive conversation and a "see you tomorrow at _____." After all, you want to make sure we know being on time isn't reserved for just our first day.

One franchisee told me how she makes the first day special, given her limited time and budget. She takes a digital picture of every new hire at the end of our first day and immediately prints it out. On the picture she writes with a colorful marker: "Jenna, congratulations on your first day! We're glad you're here. You have a big future with us!" She then gives this to the new hire as a memento along with a handshake. Remember, *anything* you can do that creates an emotional connection between a Gen Yer and your company on our first day will make the experience unforgettable and, best of all, blog-worthy.

Y-SIZE QUESTIONS

1. Do you currently do anything to make the first day stand out for a new hire?
2. Can you start new hires on a day other than Monday or on whatever day is least stressful in your workplace?
3. Is it possible for you to have even a handful of business cards ready for new hires on Day One?

CHAPTER 8

Orientation: Confirming Our Fit within Your Culture

(Or, "That slide show was frickin' hilarious. You should put it on YouTube!")

Day One rocked. You *completely* surpassed the Gen Y new hire's expectations with your *Y-Sized* tactics (and he or she already texted three friends to tell them about her new business cards). Now it's on to orientation. Your goal is simple: prove to Gen Y that we made a *good decision* by joining your company—and underscore your expectations for us in the workplace. You do this by providing as much immersion as possible into your culture, telling us about our role within the greater company, and giving us some initial direction as to where we go from here.

The challenge facing employers is producing and delivering a replicable orientation program that teaches new hires the core things we need to know—without boring us to tears (although, at least, that would mean we were still awake). The key to *Y-Size* your company's orientation, so you get consistently better results in less time, is to adjust your orientation materials and process to align with Gen Y's learning styles.

There are three big learning style elements that should be the cornerstone of your orientation planning:

- Gen Y has a *very* short attention span (think Super Bowl commercial length *minus* five seconds).
- We expect our learning to be highly interactive (Can I touch it? Pretty please? Just once?).
- We want tangible outcomes from our learning efforts (So, when can I expect my Certificate of Completion and link to our online orientation photo album?).

From a learning standpoint, my research shows that Gen Y wants short bursts of information, followed by discussion and group participation, followed by challenges with tangible outcomes. In other words, if your orientation is watching eight hours of 1992 training videos (love that green polka-dotted tie!) with a few worksheets and quizzes in between, then it's time to step it up.

For those of you who do not have a formal orientation, or want to supplement your existing orientation program, later in the chapter I will share some flexible tools you can use to get Gen Y going in the right direction, *one employee at a time*. Either way, you want your orientation to build on the excitement that a new employee feels on his or her first day. You want to showcase your culture so that we feel 100 percent confident that we made a good decision by joining your team, and you lay the foundation for our future growth and accountability once orientation is complete.

FORMAL ORIENTATIONS

Larger companies typically have some sort of formal, structured orientation program that can be easily replicated. This fits their size and situation, since they hire a lot of people, often in multiple locations, and need to repeatedly share a consistent message in a cost- and time-efficient manner. For big companies, a common solution to delivering a scalable orientation is integrating technology as the backbone of an orientation. The technology is usually implemented via a web-hosted training application or a more traditional video/teach/quiz method. While these strategies have been sufficient in the past (mainly for online defensive driving), they certainly don't play to Gen Y's learning styles (shockingly, not all of us like video games) or orientation priorities (such as meeting the good-looking girl or guy across the room).

Start with a pat on the back—from ourselves

When I talk with Gen Y, it's clear to me that we are really looking for one major thing in a new employer's orientation: We want to learn what the company is all about so that we can feel confident we've made a good employment decision. Sure, there are many things you must cover in an orientation (like no fraternizing with coworkers, which includes that good-looking person across the room), but what Gen Y wants to know by the end of orientation is what your company stands for, believes in, and works toward. *It's this emotional and logical connection that will lay the groundwork for our future loyalty—and for our desire to go above and beyond in our job performance.*

At the same time, Gen Y fully expects to learn on the job well after orientation is complete, so rather than spending 8 or 16 hours trying to cram our minds with every nugget of real-world knowledge that was not on a standardized test in high school, focus instead on having us go home at the end of each orientation day thinking "Yeah, I made a good decision to go to work here."

Breaking the ice—the first five minutes set the tone

Much as the first day at work determines whether or not a Gen Y employee considers staying with a new employer long-term, the first five minutes in an orientation program set the tone for the entire day or days. You want Gen Y participating immediately so that we don't have time to tune out. I recommend turning the tables on us right away by asking Gen Y to kick off the session by talking amongst ourselves.

The way you do this is by asking us to share something from our background or life experiences that caused us to want to work for your company. Maybe we previously shopped at your stores; maybe our parents worked at your headquarters; maybe we drove past your building every day and wandered inside to see what was going on (and what was all that noise about?). This is much more personal and engaging than the canned responses you get with, "Why did you choose to work here?" Uh, cause you have a lot of free parking (insert blank stare here).

Follow this by dividing the orientation participants into smaller groups where new hires share a variety of information with one another—at least five different things that reinforce our individuality—ranging from background and education to favorite movies or dream vacations. Remember, Gen Y wants to be seen as individuals. We also want to build a bond with the strangers around us *before* we go through a shared educational experience where we will be evaluated (especially if our scores will be recorded or displayed in front of the group). Also make sure everyone has some sort of nametag to help those of us who are "name challenged."

Corporate culture 101—mission before money

Once you've broken down some of the barriers among participants, bring your company's culture, history, mission, and values to life. You can do this by showing old video footage or photos of the company founders trying to get the company off the ground. You can also pass around examples of your earliest products, so new hires can hold them and compare them to your latest products (and probably laugh at what used to be considered high tech—like mechanical pencils). If you're a really big company, bring examples of your earliest advertisements, so we can be amused by what people used to sit through before TiVo. Also bring any other company memorabilia that gives new hires a feel for what makes your company different, meaningful, and successful.

One thing I always emphasize to orientation leaders is to focus first and foremost on your company's mission rather than on the bottom line. *Gen Yers want to see ourselves as part of a business or organization that is having an impact.* Show us what you're up to and where you're headed *before* you go into how you make money.

The specifics—make 'em stick

After giving a solid intro into what makes your company special, you can *then* go into the required training videos and instructional curriculum. I suggest, however, that if a video is more than 20 minutes long, find a way to break it up. This can be accomplished by asking questions of the participants about what we just watched, telling a story or joke related to the video clip, or my favorite: leaving a few blank places in the orientation workbook for Gen Y to write how we think something should be done (such as our own description of excellent customer service). Terra Resort Group uses this technique and has found it very engaging with their Gen Y new hires. Apparently, Gen Y likes being able to write our own version of Policies and Procedures—especially if we have to follow them!

As you go through the required learning modules, remember that Gen Y loves to be in groups—but not necessarily on teams. If you are going to use teams, decide on a transparent and random way to assemble them, such as drawing from a hat (which one of the Gen Yers surely has in his or her backpack) in front of everyone. This eliminates the perception of playing favorites, which Gen Y *really* dislikes. As much as possible, have the groups or teams take on challenges that lead to *tangible outcomes* and highlight the intended learning.

One of my favorite tactics is to ask Gen Y to present one piece of the information we were just taught in a way that people in the room find easier to understand. You might suggest we deliver the information as a skit, in an infomercial format, or as if we were a politician running for office (which is especially fun if we get to vote for our favorite pitch). This not only strengthens our learning, but also gives you ideas for making the orientation content better—and it provides some unscripted interaction, which keeps everyone's attention.

Peer-to-peer communication

New Gen Y hires need to hear from a young employee about how a Gen Yer's career might develop within your company. This person, who we will view as a more experienced peer, will be much more likely to understand our frame of reference and have recent experience dealing with the situations we are likely to face at work.

You might give this employee a few talking points ahead of time to spark an initial conversation with orientation participants and then open it up to the new hires to ask questions.

The more honest and open the dialogue, the better. I even suggest that the orientation leader should leave the room during this part of the program to encourage more candid conversation. Another option is to ask the employee to talk about what he or she thought the first year was going to be like versus what it actually was like or to share stories about two or three favorite work projects so far. You can also foster conversations like these by inviting slightly more experienced employees to have lunch with those of us going through orientation.

Eye on the ball

Have all new hires write our first-year goals with the company and the steps we will take to get there. Then have us detail different ways we will measure our progress. If your company uses a standard performance evaluation, *give this to each employee during orientation*. Then explain how and when we will be evaluated (and by whom).

By doing this, you've shown us what actions, behaviors, and outcomes are important to your organization *before* we start work. I also think you should ask us to complete our evaluation as if we were our boss and it was a year from now. This simple exercise of tying the future to the present connects where we are today with where we want to be. It also underscores that you expect us to be with your company one year from now (a message you want to keep sending). Make a photocopy of each new hire's first-year goals and give us the original to keep. Writing these goals and completing the evaluation helps new hires to clarify our direction and gives our new boss insight into some of our plans and motivations.

Lovely parting gifts I: Free stuff

At some point during the orientation, *everyone* should receive a cool T-shirt, bumper sticker, or some other SWAG (Stuff We All Get). This could be a cold drink koozie or coffee mug with a funny saying, a catchy bumper sticker with the company logo, or something else that physically signifies we are now a part of the company or even an industry within the region. The quirkier and more off-the-wall, the better.

When I was speaking to a group of oil field managers and executives, they told me the hottest accessory among their workers was a bumper sticker that read "Rockin' the Bakken," which pays tribute to the geological formation that spurred their current oil boom (there is even a web site: www.rockinthebakken.com). I can't tell you exactly what kind of kitschy things will connect with your new Gen Y employees, but I do know that the more employment branded goodies you give us, the more we will have to show our friends at Happy Hour. If you can create (or have a contest to create) SWAG with a funny saying, I guarantee we will proudly show off the results. For example, if you're in the print or online content business, you could have a T-shirt that reads "_____.com: Our writing is so good you don't need to read between the lines."

Lovely parting gifts II: A diploma

At the end of the formal orientation, give each participant a tangible outcome that signifies completion. Yes, I know that Gen Y is often disparaged for always expecting a ribbon (personally, I prefer a trophy), but we do want to leave with something that emotionally takes us back to our orientation experience. This could be a graduation photo with all the participants at the end of the final orientation day or something more creative. For instance, if we passed around examples of your company's early products, give us a replica of an early product as a keepsake. You can also challenge the orientation participants to create our own mementos representing the shared experience.

Those employers seeking to learn if a new hire is really committed to your company can follow the lead of Zappos, a company that has received tremendous media coverage for its unique approach to employment. At the end of its new employee orientation, all participants are given a choice. They can either take the job they've been offered (new employees typically start on the lowest levels and work their way up), *or they can get paid up to $2,000 not to take the job.*

No, that's not a typing error. Zappos pays people up to $2,000 *not* go to work for them after they've completed their entire orientation process. They believe if a person chooses the money over the job, then they aren't the right fit for the company. It's more in line with their culture to pay them *not* to go to work rather than bring them on as an employee who is not excited about working at their company.

Be sure to provide the orientation class with a bulleted list of learning objectives covered and, if possible, the e-mail address for each participant, in case we want to stay in touch with each other (especially the attractive person who we want to meet but not fraternize with). The end of orientation is also a great time to present new hires with business cards if you haven't already done so.

The orientation curriculum—what Gen Y needs to get from orientation

What should be in that bulleted list of learning objectives? At the close of the official orientation, your Gen Y new hires should have a basic understanding and comfort level with the following concepts:

- Culture (What does "normal" look, sound, and feel like at your company?)
- Values and Vision (What does your company stand for, and where are you headed in the next five years? How will you know when you get there? Be specific and measurable.)
- Roles and Responsibility (What are my job responsibilities? When and how will I know if I'm successful?)
- Communication (How will I stay in touch with my colleagues, boss, and company leadership?)
- Promotions and Opportunity (What are the company's growth priorities, and what do I need to do to grow with them?)
- Training, Safety, and Development (Where are the learning opportunities that will help me maximize my value as a professional inside and outside of work?)
- Ethics and Accountability (How does the company determine what is ethical, and who holds us accountable?)
- Respect and Leadership (What does a respectful work environment look like and how do our leaders model the behaviors they want to see in the company?)

ONE-OF-A-KIND, ONE-AT-A-TIME ORIENTATION

Due to size, resources, or operational model, many businesses don't have (or don't need) a large-scale, formal orientation program. If this fits your situation, or you want to supplement an existing orientation program, there are three self-paced and flexible steps you can take to make an individual new hire feel like he or she is off to a good start, *thanks to you.*

Step 1: The Unofficial First 30 Handbook, or Top 30 Tips for Your First 30 Days

Every company has some type of employee handbook or manual outlining its Policies and Procedures that new hires are supposed to read, learn, and abide by. While this manual can be helpful (mainly for putting us to sleep), and is often a legal necessity, it doesn't always convey the most important information that a new Gen Y employee needs (such as the type of sandals that are actually considered "business casual"—if there are any). If you want to give us a printed document that has real value to us from the moment we start our new job, provide us with a *First 30 Handbook.*

This is my favorite resource for orientation, whether you have 20,000 employees or only two (which means it's even more important that they get off to a good start). A *First 30 Handbook* reveals behind-the-scenes insights that new hires will find extraordinarily valuable and practical (such as the five closest lunch places that are good, fast, and cheap). We won't find this information listed in any formal Policies and Procedures manual. You develop this priceless resource in true Gen Y style—with user-generated content—by asking current Gen Y employees to create it based on their experiences working for your company. Simply put, you send an e-mail to employees who have less than three years experience asking them some version of the following question: "What is one thing we should have told you or taught you that would have made your first year on the job easier or more effective?"

You'll get answers such as:

Even though they say be here around 8:30 AM, apparently 9:00 AM is not "around 8:30 AM."

Casual Friday doesn't mean sweat pants.

When they say no pets allowed, they mean even small pets, like gerbils.

If the copier breaks, don't bother calling IT. Go find John on the 2nd floor.
    He can fix it.

It's okay to make mistakes. We all do. But make the same mistake three
    times and management will view hiring you as the mistake.

I wish I would've known I had to go to work when it was snowing.

That last answer is one of my favorites. Clearly she grew up in south Texas.

Some essential topics to include in the unofficial handbook:

- Mass transit suggestions (including lack thereof);
- Technical resources;
- Food and drink recommendations;
- Attire no-no's;
- Compensation and benefits explanations (How come they take money out of my paycheck *before* I even get it?);
- Housing must-see's; and
- Recreation options (traditional and nontraditional. Think Frisbee golf and yoga mats).

Please don't underestimate the importance of the *First 30 Handbook*. One Gen Y employee I interviewed had his car towed on his first day at work because he parked in the wrong place. Both he and his boss were embarrassed (and I'm sure the person he borrowed the car from was peeved, too). Remember, workplace circumstances change rapidly. Keep your handbook from becoming outdated by regularly re-evaluating your *First 30 Handbook*.

Step 2: Help us connect the dots

Once a Gen Y new hire has the inside track on "the way things are done around here," show us where we fit within the company's overall operations. We need to see why our job is important and how much you're *depending on us* to make an immediate impact. There are many creative ways to do this besides showing us an org chart that looks like Mt. Everest (our spot being just below base camp).

My personal favorite is a new hire scavenger hunt. To do this, give the new hire a description of the things he or she is to find, which could range from where raw materials arrive to where marketing materials are created, and tell him or her to take a picture with them. Then ask us to map the operational process by putting all these pictures in the order of operations, from start to finish. Once that is complete, ask us to explain our place in the system and what happens if we, or our departments, don't do our jobs correctly. Don't just tell us we are important. *Let us see for ourselves* (and take the pictures to prove it).

Step 3: Let us learn the ropes from someone who knows

The most intense way I know to get individual new hires up to speed fast is for us to apprentice or shadow current employees in a career path we are to eventually take on, especially those employees who started on the ground floor and worked their way up. While the concept of apprenticing has been around a very long time (think: Knights of the Round Table era) and is still considered normal in some cultures, the idea of learning by following a more experienced employee is often not used to full advantage.

To make an apprenticeship as valuable as possible, provide the apprentice with resource preparation material in advance. This material should describe the position they are to learn about and the top accountabilities for the job. The more baseline knowledge we have before we start the apprenticeship, the faster we will grow into the position.

Eliminate misunderstandings before they happen. At the beginning of the apprenticeship, make sure the experienced employee clearly shares his or her expectations with the apprentice, along with any safety rules, and then asks the apprentice for his or her expectations. Both the apprentice and the experienced employee should agree on how the apprentice will document the learning process and when he or she will be able to demonstrate newly developed skills in order to take on more responsibility. The idea is not for apprentices to simply watch, but to gradually take on more responsibility so that they can eventually move forward in their career path without their guru (i.e., the experienced employee can go on a bathroom break without everything falling apart).

Chefs at upscale restaurants utilize the apprentice system well. Chefs-in-training at fancy restaurants start out at the very bottom of the totem pole (i.e., barely above dishwasher, and I do mean barely, even if they have a fancy culinary degree). They are assigned the most elementary tasks, preparing ingredients for different dishes under the watchful eye of more experienced chefs. Gradually the apprentices are given new and greater responsibilities, but only after they have demonstrated mastery of the less exacting tasks.

One benefit to using an apprenticeship model, whether in a high-pressure kitchen or in a low-pressure sales environment, is that the Gen Y employee finds out very quickly if he or she has what it takes to make it in that job. While most managers are certainly not going to yell and throw food and cookware at an apprentice (at least not like Gordon Ramsay would do), an "orientation by apprenticeship" approach does push new hires to figure out *fast* if they can rise to the level necessary to succeed in their new job. Or, as Chef Ramsay might say, "Yes, you can cut a carrot wrong, and you just did!" (I think I would last about three minutes in his kitchen—and that was if I was in charge of the microwave!)

Step 4: Immerse us in the business

When you are leading an orientation for one, involve a new hire in as much of the traditional business experience as quickly as possible. Let us sit in on meetings relevant to our new position, listen in on conference calls, and even join you for a business lunch (but let us know ahead of time, because we never carry cash).

Alaskan Brewing does this well—and in doing so meets their safety requirements. Every new employee is introduced to the brewery through an in-depth plant-wide safety tour. The company then builds on this initial exposure by offering all employees, no matter their department, the opportunity to learn as much about the brewing process as they would like. They can cross-train as a brewer for two weeks or shadow a brewer for a day, serve on their daily quality assurance taste panel (I want that job!), or even work toward becoming a nationally certified beer judge. Employees can even learn about non-production jobs by cross-training in marketing, maintenance, accounting, or even IT.

Ashley Johnston, communications manager for Alaskan Brewing Co., explained it to me this way: "We all work better as a company team when we understand not just our job, but how our job affects the others." My favorite part of the Alaskan Brewing employment experience: Each employee has the opportunity to make his or her own homemade brew at the company. Some of these are so good they get turned into actual brands. Now, *that* is a vote of confidence in our future (and our taste buds).

When it comes to orientation, Gen Y wants and needs to soak up your company's employment experience. Everything else in our lives has been interactive, fast-paced, and hands-on, and the best new-employee orientations are, too. You will know your orientation has effectively risen to this challenge when we are instantly able to explain what makes your culture special, how we fit within the culture, and which direction we are headed to make a difference within the company.

Once you've designed an orientation that meets our learning styles (and we've uploaded and tagged our orientation group photos on Flickr), then it's time to get us engaged at work and keep us focused on meeting your desired results.

Y-SIZE QUESTIONS

1. Does your orientation process have at least three interactive components?
2. How soon can you create a *First 30 Handbook* or a similar behind-the-scenes reference document?
3. What tangible outcome does your orientation create that Gen Y employees get to keep?

CHAPTER 9

Keep Gen Y Engaged @ Work

(Or, Employee engagement doesn't mean dating your coworker.)

I thought I had prepared myself for the experience. I was wrong. Completely wrong. Walking into Hot Topic's national headquarters took my breath away. To my left were burning candles and faded pictures, a shrine to dead musicians. Near the shrine were small meeting rooms, each with a different theme. My favorite was the surgery room—complete with IV bag holder—where the employees met to "fix things." Directly in front of me were two enthusiastic receptionists, a bit younger than myself, who had some very cool (and prominent) tattoos, exciting hair colors, and interesting piercings. That alone would be enough to give most executives a hot flash, especially if your company was publicly held and generated more than $700 million annually. However, at Hot Topic this was *normal*.

Behind the receptionists was a huge set of shelves filled with rock and roll regalia. All around me music was blaring (even in the parking lot!) and TVs were flashing music-related videos. The energy in the building was palpable. To say entering Hot Topic headquarters was spellbinding would be an understatement, but it is a fitting and stimulating environment for a market-leading retailer of all things music-related whose primary customer is Gen Y.

My adventure was only beginning. Jerome, a Hot Topic executive ("executive" being one of the Seven Dirty Words you're taught not to say inside the company), greeted me and complimented my decision to wear jeans and an untucked short-sleeve shirt. Apparently, tucked in shirts are a no-no, and showing up in a tie might lead to it being cut off—while you're wearing it. Jerome then asked if I was "ready to experience Hot Topic." Never had an executive asked me a question like that—especially on a company tour. Good thing he did. When he opened the small door to the massive room behind the oversized shelves, I felt like I'd been transported behind the Wizard's curtain.

Welcome to Oz. (Toto, I have a feeling we're not in Kansas any more.)

In front of me stretched desks and people as far as I could see. (I later learned more than 470 people worked in the one vast warehouse-style space). Jerome explained that Hot Topic does not believe in cubicles, or assistants, or really anything else that can divide employees. In fact, employees do not have titles listed on their business cards, not even the CEO!

Walking through the maze of desks, people were talking everywhere. Some were sitting on couches in the middle of the room; others were dialoguing one-on-one over their desks or on their cell phones as they walked around, simultaneously waving across the room for someone to come over. Everywhere I went, the music was pulsating and TVs and computer screens were flashing.

I couldn't miss all the colors. The clothing samples were every color imaginable, along with many in black (which is always popular in LA and NYC). The employees, too, wore a variety of clothing styles (not to mention multiple piercings and tattoos) that would give many a conservative parent a fit. As we walked through the maze, I got to tour the amphitheater-style auditorium *in the center of the office*—where bands play—as well as visit a room with white-boards on every wall.

And then I was introduced to Betsy McLaughlin, Hot Topic's CEO, whose desk I'd already walked past twice. I would have never known she was the CEO because she had the same desk and setup as everyone else; in fact, when I met her, she was booking her own airline tickets!

Interviewing Betsy in the middle of this energy-filled room, I couldn't help but be drawn into the culture that makes Hot Topic so special—and so brilliantly engages its Gen Y employees. Betsy told me that when she became CEO, it was never her intention to foster a company culture that Gen Y loves (imagine talking on your cell phone at your desk, getting every other Friday off due to flex schedules, and having bands play in your own office!). She said she simply wanted to support a culture where people could express themselves and stay true to what Hot Topic stands for: Everything About the Music.

The most impressive part of my Hot Topic tour was watching *how hard* the employees worked to build on the company's tremendous success. They did this in spite of all the factors many employers tell me they fear most (Gen Y talking on cell phones at work, playing music on our computers, no cubicles or corner offices, dress code gone wild, etc.). What I learned from Betsy, and saw in action, was that rather than Gen Y playing video games at work or spending all day chatting with friends on Facebook (both of which you can do at Hot Topic), Gen Y employees rise to the challenge to deliver results for the company. They are truly engaged in their work, know their coworkers are counting on them, and make it happen.

This, to me, is the essence of Gen Y engagement: *Knowing your culture, employees, and mission well enough that you can lead employees to do the right things at the right time with the right mindset toward results (even if Pearl Jam is playing in the background).*

Many executives I work with chuckle at the idea of approaching Gen Y employee engagement in the way Hot Topic does. I understand why, and recognize that Hot Topic's approach is certainly not for everyone. You probably don't have the latest music blasting in your parking lot, a wall signed by visiting bands, or a shrine to dead musicians (with Michael Jackson now, sadly, included). However, you can find meaningful insight in the culture Betsy has fostered by simply recognizing that with the right leadership, Gen Y, despite our reputation, can be engaged, hard-working employees. I think it's also worth noting that Betsy's employees range in age from teenagers to beyond the age of 60, and not surprisingly, they work very well together.

Engaged Gen Y employees are driven to do their best to achieve the specific outcomes most important to *you* and *your company* at that time. This is also the ideal mindset for Gen Y to deliver discretionary effort. By discretionary effort, I mean doing more than the minimum required to get a job done correctly. This is the fabled "above and beyond" performance level, where companies really move forward. And, yes, this is possible. I've seen it—and at companies much less edgy or high-tech than Hot Topic.

At most companies, you can tell you've successfully engaged a Gen Y employee when we're not stretching a 15-minute break into 30 minutes (which we justify by saying we went to the bathroom *after* our break was over) or chatting with a coworker about our latest adventures in online dating rather than doing our job. An engaged Gen Y employee is focused on our company's current objectives and constantly thinking about ways we can better meet them. *The more engaged the employee, the more valuable we are to you.* It's the difference between paying a Gen Yer for eight hours of work and us only working six hours. Those two hours of wages you paid us for, but we did not earn, become expensive quickly. Not only do they cost you our wages and associated expenses, but you also lost opportunity.

The challenge inherent in keeping Gen Y engaged is that we're easily distracted, we want to see progress from our daily efforts, and we have a high need to stay in touch with those leading us (what Gen X calls "both high maintenance *and* annoying"). With a little *Y-Sizing*, however, these potential engagement obstacles can become big assets in your workplace, helping you to achieve greater results with fewer resources because we are more effectively using our time. In fact, when you successfully engage Gen Y, you will likely gain the added benefit of engaging your other employees, too (because we will stop bothering them with our online trivia questions).

TURNING GEN Y @ WORK INTO
GEN WOW @ WORK

Most managers I interview will admit that when Gen Y is excited about a task or outcome, we can work really, really hard to make it happen. However, the same managers will also say that Gen Y can just as easily drift to the other end of the performance spectrum when we are disinterested in the work at hand—meaning we show up *at work* but we don't actually show up *to work*.

This peaks-and-valleys performance range especially frustrates older generations who are counting on us to perform consistently. One Baby Boomer manager put it to me this way: "Back when I was starting out, if a younger person was told to do something at work, we just did it, no questions asked. Our boss didn't have to explain why we were to do something, or have an award ceremony for us after we did it. If we were supposed to take out the trash, we took out the trash. We felt lucky to have a job, let alone one that paid a decent wage. It seems your generation wants us to feel lucky that we have them."

While I don't entirely agree with this manager's statement (although I've heard it *so* many times I'm at risk of believing it), I do know that Boomers and Matures were raised to believe that doing a good job was important to their self-worth, no matter how menial the task or the pay. Gen Y, on the other hand, doesn't automatically bring that same sense of pride and responsibility to every work-related task, especially lower-skilled but necessary tasks like sweeping the floor or filing papers. However, that doesn't mean you can't manage us in a way that makes us *want* to do a good job, regardless of a task's perceived glory. The key is to make the right kind of connection with us when it comes to positioning the task.

After interviewing many Gen Y employees, I propose a three-fold approach that provides a foundation for our engagement. Once we're paying attention, you can then build on this foundation using the actions described later in this chapter. This combination will help Gen Y stay engaged, even when our friends text message us to leave work because they got "sick" and are now headed to the lake. (Must be seasickness . . .)

Here's the process to build a foundation for Gen Y employee engagement:

- Step 1: Reposition tasks as challenges
- Step 2: Ask for our opinion
- Step 3: Turn monotony into a victory

Step 1: Going from task to challenge

Businesses run on basic tasks being performed correctly and consistently over and over again. These are the daily activities that *must* happen for a business to continue operating and could range from answering customer calls or processing orders to prepping files for a legal case. These repetitious but essential tasks often fall to Gen Y, especially when we are the lowest paid or least experienced segment of your employee base. To get us engaged in these seemingly menial tasks, be it sharpening pencils or some other tearfully boring but essential assignment (Wow, I get to scan *all* 6,738 of your business cards! Thanks!), the first step is *to turn the task into a challenge.*

To do this, reposition big, boring monotonous tasks as bite-size performance challenges with near-term results. How? It's all in the presentation.

Instead of saying, "Please put these 500 client folders in alphabetical order" (and seeing us hit Play on our iPod before we get started), reposition the task as a tiny daily or weekly challenge. You could say, "How fast do you think you can alphabetize these client folders without error?" or "If it really was urgent, how soon do you think you could alphabetize these client folders?"

Now you've made us look past the monotony (and color-coded alphabet soup), and you have us thinking about the desired outcome and our role in creating it. When you reposition a task so that we focus on the outcome rather than the repetition, we will get the job done ASAP—and time ourselves doing it (based on the number of songs we listened to on our playlist).

Step 2: Ask our opinion

You can take this approach to another level by asking us for our opinion about how to do the task faster and better next time. "Once you've alphabetized these files, I'd like to hear any ideas you have on how we could make this entire process more efficient next week."

With that one simple question, you've totally caught us off guard, empowered us to have a voice, and *pushed us to think about solutions* while doing something that would normally require little thought (except dreaming about all the other places we'd rather be). This forces us to consider how to work smarter, not harder, to make a process better, and also to see unglamorous tasks as mini-projects. Perhaps best of all, it also gives us the interaction and sense of perceived importance that we crave.

Let's imagine you need a Gen Y employee to sweep the floor of your business. Nothing fancy about the task, but it has to be done— and probably on a regular basis. Rather than telling your most junior employee, "John, please go sweep the floor," and watching John trudge off in defeat (using the broom as either a crutch or hockey stick), consider saying it this way: "Hi John. I need you to sweep the floor, *but* I know you have a bigger future at our company than being a floor sweeper. So while you're sweeping the floor, I'd like you to think of ways we can keep the floor from getting so dirty all the time or ways to make it easier to clean next time. Your ideas could really help us out."

While some of our ideas may be completely unworkable (such as, "Don't let customers walk inside"), I think you might be surprised by the creativity of some of them ("If we gave each customer half the napkins we do now, most of which end up unused on the floor anyway, then we'd automatically keep our floor cleaner"). Actually, you shouldn't be surprised at all; you've just asked an expert. The Gen Y employee you've asked to sweep the floor for the 37th time has already spent a lot of hours looking down and wishing he could find a way to do something more important—such as track down the person who leaves nine unused napkins under a table in a slanted teepee formation.

Step 3: Rethinking monotony

My favorite way to turn monotony into victory is to take a larger project or initiative and divide it into smaller projects with clear, ongoing, or measurable outcomes, preferably daily outcomes. Rather than saying, "I need one hundred data points on the topic

of _____ presented in this form _____ by Friday."You could say
"I need 25 data points on the topic of _____ presented in this
form _____ every day by 5:00 PM for the next four days." Same
end result, *but you've made it a daily goal* rather than allowing us to
procrastinate until the end of the week (which means you get better
results *and* we stay focused). Remember, whatever you tell us you're
going to measure is where we will focus our efforts. And what gets
measured gets managed.

After you've helped a Gen Yer turn the seemingly boring
task of stamping 500 envelopes into a Stamp-A-Thon Challenge,
you're now ready to keep us feeling connected to you, our other
colleagues, and other company leaders without becoming our
BFF.

COMMUNICATION: FROM HIGH MAINTENANCE TO HIGH FIDELITY

One of the biggest frustrations I hear from employers (and yes,
I hear *many* of their frustrations, but that's simply part of the
improvement process) is that Gen Y is high-maintenance and
needy. They say we want constant attention (who *me*?) and that
we can't seem to do much without asking someone else's opinion
first ("I don't know if I agree with that statement; let me ask my
dad.") As a member of Gen Y, I completely understand why many
employers feel the way they do about us. I'm guilty of wanting
lots of communication. I like feedback, staying in touch with the
people on my team, and asking those I respect if they think I'm
making good decisions.

So maybe Gen Y is a *little* needier than other generations (or at
least we are willing to voice our questions when other generations
weren't), but another way of looking at it is that maybe some of us
simply don't want to waste time doing the wrong thing. We also
don't have the work experience to always know what to do next,
and we gain confidence and comfort knowing that there are people
we can count on.

Okay, now that I've tried my best to justify my own need for
ongoing communication and attention, let me show you how to
make this an advantage for your company.

COMMUNICATE WITH BITS OF INFORMATION

My conversations with executives reveal that when they say Gen Y is high-maintenance and needy, it's not that they are saying we are difficult in the diva sense of the word. We don't ask for a confetti party in our cubicle or gold-embossed business cards (One with our picture on it will do just fine). *It's that we simply expect more communication than our boss is accustomed to giving.* This is particularly true with Boomer bosses, who generally feel that if employees are doing a good job, you should stay out of their way and focus on those who aren't meeting expectations.

Most of the communication pressure that bosses feel from Gen Y employees is dissolved the moment they recognize that Gen Y doesn't want tons of detailed information, just small bits of information delivered *with more frequency*—perhaps much more frequency. We don't want a three-page memo with footnotes or a weekly PowerPoint presentation with accompanying reference materials. Both of those sound absolutely terrible to read (or sleep) through.

All we want is a five second check-in from you by e-mail, text, or in person once a week. We simply want to know that you took a moment (literally) to make sure we are included, informed, up-to-date, and acknowledged. All you have to do is stop us in the hallway or outside our cubicle, and say, "Hi Sam. Good work helping Mrs. Lee." That's it. No group hug singing "Kumbaya," or Tony Robbins-style walk-on-fire rally in the employee break room. Just notice us for five seconds a week and save yourself hours of perceived neediness down the road.

One of my most charismatic Fortune 500 executive clients inadvertently proved this to me and to himself while attempting to prove me wrong. During a conference call he told me, "Jason, I have to be honest with you. I thought you were full of it when you talked about the importance of taking a second to acknowledge Gen Y employees at work. So I decided to prove you wrong (which is not a shock coming from this particular executive). I took a different path to my office every morning this week. Whenever I walked past a Gen Yer typing away in his or her cubicle, I said, 'Hello' or 'Good to see you.' Damn, if they didn't love it! They got so excited. I couldn't believe it. It was like I was giving away free candy to eight-year-olds.

If I were in their shoes, I would *never* want my boss sticking his head in my cubicle unannounced. But they responded like I was giving them a promotion, and all I said was 'hello' as I passed by. I didn't get it, but I believe it now."

RULES OF ENGAGEMENT

Once you have figured out how often you can comfortably communicate with your Gen Y employees, it's time to set clear ground rules for engaged communication. These rules may seem childish to set up, but we do well when given a few boundaries and a lot of freedom within them (kind of like curfew, but without sharing the same house). In addition, these rules will save you from confusing late-night phone calls as we try to find out your ideal cover sheet font size:

Rule 1. Who to contact if we have a problem.

We shouldn't call the CEO for help just because someone played a joke on us by changing our voicemail greeting and instructions into Portuguese (although whoever did that to us is pretty darn funny). We should know to call a more experienced coworker, read the *First 30 Handbook,* or send our direct supervisor a specific e-mail with an explanation of the problem in the subject line. I recommend sharing the following creed with your Gen Y employees: Day-to-day problems should be handled by your day-to-day boss.

Rule 2. Hours when you can be reached and how.

This is very important, because if you don't set boundaries, we will abide by our own normal communication preferences, which means text, call, e-mail, or drop by your office (and possibly your home) any time we've had inspiration and a Red Bull.

To get this point across, I would go with something like, "You can call until 8 PM and text until 10 PM, but don't make my phone vibrate after *The Daily Show* has started."

However, if it's an emergency (and explain what that means), don't hesitate to call anytime. Your willingness to be there when we need you the most strengthens our loyalty to you and can lead to some entertaining phone calls (starting with a message about accepting the collect calling fees).

Rule 3. Communicate to get the best and most accurate response.

Gen Y communicates differently than other generations. You know what works best for you, so tell us. We know what works best for us, so let us share. Have a conversation and find a middle ground where you're comfortable with a compromise, or simply tell us specifically how you want the information presented (especially if you want it in complete sentences). Understand that if you like handwritten notes, then we'll print you a note in script. If you like e-mail, we'll use that, but if you don't like text messages, you must let us know ASAP. Otherwise we might be sending you important messages and your 12-year-old daughter may be reading them! Once you've told us how to communicate with you, you've also created a situation in which you have every right to hold us accountable to that standard.

GOING BEYOND THE BASICS

To create an even deeper level of engagement, use these nontraditional *Y-Size* communication ideas:

Be the 411

When breaking news happens at your business, be the one who tells us. You do this by e-mailing us when something big goes down, such as our division receiving a fantastic customer service review. You announce this via e-mail by only writing in the subject line: "We got a 9.7 on our CSR!!! Chocolate chip cookies on me!" If your business model doesn't support communicating en masse by e-mail, create a cell phone number list so that you can send a text message to your entire team all at once. Something to which you should alert the team: "We just closed our biggest sale ever! Recession? We don't believe in no recession!" (Any messages like that will boost morale in tough times.)

Just make sure not to send junk text messages. In our view, they are worse than e-mail spam, because we have to manually delete them. Send us the news and nothing but the news. Hint: If you text us at 4 AM, be ready to expect an immediate reply.

Linda LoRe, president and CEO of Frederick's of Hollywood, has approximately 1,000 employees staffing the firm's retail stores; 84 percent of them are in Gen Y. Since her business depends so heavily on Gen Y employees, she makes it a point to know how to best keep them engaged at work. This is particularly important, since she may only have one or two employees working in a store at any given time.

One realization she had is that her Gen Y employees wanted to hear directly from her—and not in a canned way—so that they feel they have the inside scoop on what's happening at headquarters and where the company is headed. Her solution: record a personal message, which is anything but corporate, that is then distributed to all her stores through the company phone system. Not only does she leave the message herself, but when her Gen Y employees do something great, they can leave *her* a message—which she then talks about!

Linda says, "I find the messages not only help me connect on a more personal level with my Gen Y employees, but ultimately they lead to an increased sense of morale and motivation." She goes on to say, "After a high-stress selling season, such as Valentine's Day or Christmas, being able to personally tell them that lunch is on me in honor of their success really makes a difference."

Weekly what's up

One of the most effective Gen Y engagement strategies I've come across is used by Melody Lentsch, an executive at the advertising firms Preston Kelly and Flipside Marketing. Melody believes that employees need face time with their boss if they are to stay engaged. Her solution was to create a weekly 30-minute meeting with *each* of her direct reports—of all ages and titles—one on one. She divides this weekly meeting into three segments. The first 10 minutes are reserved for the employees to talk about any subjects they want. During the next 10 minutes, Melody does the talking. For the final 10 minutes, the employee and Melody talk about the employee's future. She does this *every* week. She has found that this consistent, predictable interaction is a huge hit with her Gen Y employees. They want to be able to share their perspective, learn on a regular basis how they are doing, and then talk about how their actions today connect with their future.

In the loop update

If Melody's weekly meetings seem like *way* too much commitment for you or your organization, shift responsibility for ongoing communication with Gen Y to Gen Y through an In the Loop Update.

Since Gen Y is so hungry to stay in the loop at work (which is why we can't stop looking at our cell phones), *let us become the loop.* Ask us to take charge of a weekly or biweekly employee-generated e-mail update, blog posting, or Intranet announcement. All you do is ask the Gen Y employee who seems most interested in staying up to date on company-related stuff (the Gen Yer who is constantly walking around the office asking people what they're doing is an excellent candidate) to send out an e-mail to other employees who want to stay in the loop.

These employees reply with a two or three sentence update about what they've been working on that week (or whatever period of time takes place between updates). The employees can share a project they're working on, a breakthrough they've had, a problem they're struggling with, or whatever else is on their minds. They can also ask for help if they are in need of something specific, such as a particular type of resource ("Anyone know of a web site that does _____?" or "Has anyone dealt with this problem before?").

These individual e-mail updates are due to the person in charge of coordinating them by a certain time every week, say Friday at 10 AM. Then the designated "In the Loop" coordinator combines these into one e-mail and circulates it to those who participated or expressed an interest in receiving the update. Depending on the coordinator's level of tech skill, they could include workplace photos, customer feedback, company news, or management's review of the past week's performance. Gen Y employees will read this e-mail with great enthusiasm because we've contributed to its creation, because it's a bit informal—which makes it credible—and because it could vary dramatically from week to week. (As an added bonus, it's considered "work," which means it's something we can work on after 4 PM on Fridays.)

Communicating electronically on a regular basis can also save you a lot of money. One of my clients heard me speak about the different ways to electronically keep Gen Y employees engaged through ongoing internal communications. She asked what I thought about the high-gloss magazine that they *physically mailed* to their employees every quarter. I couldn't help but ask, "So . . . you mean my mom would get it?"

They scrapped the printed version and replaced it with an electronic version, which instantly saved the company more than $20,000 in production costs *per issue!* They also tapped into a whole new generation of readers who had never seen the magazine before. (I'm sure, however, that some of our parents are now disappointed their free subscription has stopped.)

If the weekly e-mail update is too much, I saw another variation I liked at a company I visited. At this company they print weekly company-related announcements on one page of paper and post them where everyone can read it: on the mirror in the bathroom! Yep, when you are washing your hands, taped to the mirror in front of you is an announcement page with a current statistic that reinforces the value of the company's mission, a news piece such as an introduction to a new employee, and important dates about upcoming product releases. Informative and sanitary.

HOW AM I DOING? THE PERFORMANCE REVIEW

Performance reviews are the critical last piece to keeping Gen Y engaged (that, or holding our cell phones for ransom). These outcome-driven interactions are what keep Gen Y focused and on task, because we know that the results we are creating will be discussed in the near future. It's my belief that if you want to keep us engaged on an ongoing basis, then you should give us performance reviews at least once a month. Otherwise we think you're holding out on us.

Melody Lentsch, whose story I shared earlier in this chapter, said it to me this way: "Gen Y does not like to hear that they've been doing something wrong for six months, but you didn't tell them because 'it wasn't review time yet.' They want constructive feedback right away, because they want to get better. This actually works in an employer's favor, because it means your employees get better, faster."

Given the importance Gen Y places on receiving feedback (especially when we are new to the workforce or to a particular employer), it's interesting that performance reviews are one of the least utilized tools for increasing our engagement. In fact, many managers I speak with think performance reviews are a waste of time, *and for good reason*. If performance reviews are not conducted in the right way, *they are a waste of time* for everyone involved. However, when you conduct them in a *Y-Size* way, performance reviews should take less than 10 minutes and lead you to see more of the actions you want from your Gen Y employees—immediately.

Here's how to make your performance reviews a top performer:

- *Change the name* from employee review or employee evaluation or any other variation of "You're Being Judged" to either perform-ance review or my favorite, talent management review (TMR). This reframes the conversation *before* it starts.
- When we take a job, have us *review and agree up front on the criteria* by which we will be evaluated in a given position. These criteria should be the same for each employee in that position. This uni-formity is what makes the process fair and helps us to understand (rather than get upset) when someone in our same position gets promoted and we don't.
- *Focus on no more than five to seven critical accountabilities for each job position.* More than seven and everyone loses interest, including the person leading the review.
- *Tie these accountabilities to specific outcomes* you want to see in your business. It's these outcomes that you review during your conver-sation, not the responsibilities.
- *Hold each TMR in private*, and start by giving the Gen Y employee a personal scorecard for the current review period. Essentially you take the top accountabilities and rate them on some matrix from outstanding to underperforming. Then, walk us through the list in the same way each time. That way we know what to expect before we start our review.
- *Most important, stick to a regular review schedule.* If you are sched-uled to meet with the employee the third Friday every month, then meet the third Friday every month. The first time you miss a meeting, you lose credibility by showing the employee that either they or the review are not really important to you.
- Make your recommendations and constructive feedback *personal, actionable, and specific.* Avoid generic clichés and give us at most two things that you want us to focus on before the next review. In other words, don't send us "back to the drawing board," because we've never had one.
- To make sure we understand what you want us to do differently before the next review, ask us to *write down on our scorecard the one or two things you most want to see improved.* Make a copy of this so that both you and the employee retain a copy for reference during the next meeting.

- *Always start and end with something positive.* This is common sense, but Gen Y is often not good at handling constructive criticism, so a little strategic communication makes the news that we didn't get an A+ a little easier to handle (and keeps mom from calling).

Y-SIZE QUESTIONS

1. What is an ongoing, repetitive but important task that you can turn into a challenge?
2. What is a communication strategy you've adopted this year that seems to really connect with Gen Y?
3. Do you have top accountabilities for each position at your company or for each position you supervise? If so, how often do you conduct performance reviews using them?

CHAPTER 10

Develop Gen Y Talent by Making "Good Enough" Unacceptable

(Or, "I can do anything I set my mind to, which is exactly why I don't.")

As you can tell from earlier chapters (and, likely, your own observation), Gen Y has much to learn about work *after* we've started. The reasons are obvious and generational. Gen Y is entering the workforce later than previous generations (Thanks, Visa!). We also get much less (if any) career education in high school or college (Thanks, No Child Left Behind!). At the same time, Gen Y has more post-secondary education than any previous generation—and the college debt to prove it.

The tradeoff is that although we may be able to recite all the steps in a customer's standard buying cycle, we may have never actually sold anything to a customer face-to-face. (And trust me, it's a *lot* different in person than on paper.) This means we can pass a test on *how* to sell, yet have no actual experience *doing* it. This creates all kinds of potential conflict—and the need for additional talent development. Why? Because we enter the workforce thinking we already have the skills that put us at the top of our game, *when in practice we still have much to learn.* (I've found this to be true for Gen Yers with high school, college, and advanced degrees.) As any experienced business leader will tell you, it's the *real-world application* of our knowledge that is most valuable to our employer and our career. The good news is that we have the raw talent and ambition (including a desire to prove ourselves, comfort with technology, entrepreneurial mindset, etc.); we just need someone to unlock the true value of what we can bring to the workplace.

One company that has proven you can systemically develop Gen Y talent—and reap the bottom-line rewards—is Enterprise Rent-A-Car. They are one of the largest employers of new college grads in the United States, and they develop their new hire talent *fast*. In fact, Enterprise makes it a point to let new hires know that their career advancement is dependent on how fast they develop their on-the-job talent, specifically learning the business' operations, taking responsibility for the outcomes they create, and treating their rental location as if it is their own business. The key to Enterprise's talent development success is their Management Training (MT) program. Here's how it works:

All new hires start with an intensive one-week classroom-style course where they learn the ins and outs of the Enterprise business model. Once the class finishes, the new hires are placed in Enterprise branches, where their rate of promotion is tied directly to how fast they master different elements of the business. The MTs do this by learning hands-on the front end of the business (such as customer service), the back end of the business (such as controlling branch costs), as well as business strategy (such as branch marketing). Each MT is rigorously assessed through a variety of metrics ranging from customer evaluations to knowledge of specific functions. The goal of the MT program is for the participant to learn *every* aspect of running an Enterprise branch in preparation for them to eventually manage their own rental branch.

How fast can Gen Y move forward with Enterprise? New hires typically complete the MT program in 8 to 12 months, depending on their scores and motivation. The next big promotion: assistant manager, which means a percentage of the Gen Yer's income is based on the bottom-line performance of their branch. This can happen in as little as 12 to 18 months from the time they are first hired. As one Enterprise executive told me, "Gen Y is willing to work really hard to develop their talent once they know what you want them to do, how it figures into the larger operation, and why it's important. When you can connect these dots, they are willing to go above and beyond for you and their career."

In addition to quickly developing Gen Y talent, Enterprise gets a nice recruiting benefit. They are frequently rated as one of the best places for Gen Y to launch our careers. Now that is a double win! Not only does Enterprise develop Gen Y talent quickly and gain the operational benefit, talented Gen Yers seek *it* out.

Whether you and your company choose to develop Gen Y talent systematically, which is what Enterprise does, or leave talent development to individual managers or departments, one thing is for certain: Gen Y employees must learn early that our value to your company— and our likelihood of promotion—is heavily reliant on our *continuous* professional learning and growth. By sending this message loud and clear (a la Jim Cramer, without the Post-It note on your forehead) you've aligned our interests with yours—so that both of us increase in value while the company moves ahead.

THE MOST IMPORTANT TALENT DEVELOPMENT MESSAGE: "GOOD ENOUGH" .... ISN'T

This is the message that should take center stage in your Gen Y talent development initiatives: "Good enough" will not get us where we want to be. "Good enough" will not lead to a promotion or raise or more prestigious responsibilities. "Good enough" will not garner the respect of company leadership. When Gen Y recognizes that "good enough" is unacceptable in relation to where we want to be, *then* we will focus our attention on the ways that we can become more valuable to you, our employer, by developing our talent. The reason: We will finally see the connection between our career goal and learning necessary skills to get there. As I always tell Gen Y young professionals in my seminars, "The way you get promoted is to show management that you're more valuable than your current position." That's when management recognizes we're ready for a chance to make a bigger impact (and earn a business card on thicker card stock).

DON'T CODDLE ME, TRAIN ME

While on-the-job training is not unusual in the United States (unlike other countries), the difference between Gen Y and older employees is that *we might need our training to start on a more basic level* and then ramp up quickly (this despite the Wall of Honors in our childhood home). At the very least, business leaders can't assume we have core competencies in all the major professional skill areas.

After all, we haven't actually been working. We've been *studying* about work. While we may be able to design a virtual universe in SimCity between 4 AM and 6 AM, we might not be able to speak in front of an audience of 30 people for 20 minutes straight. We also might not be able to leave a voicemail message that makes a client actually want to call us back. At the same time, we may have a brilliant solution for dramatically improving internal company communication. (If only we thought to tell you about it rather than bemoan how badly the current system operates.) The good news is that with only a little effort—and some *Y-Size* strategies—you can begin to develop Gen Y employee talent without expensive training and without disrupting your ongoing operations.

I recommend you start by assessing your organization's Gen Y talent development needs. You can do so by answering the following questions:

1. What are the most common job responsibilities for a current Gen Y employee in your company? What skills must Gen Y master to be a leader in that position?

_____

_____

These skills are your short-term talent development objectives.

2. What will be the most common job responsibilities for a Gen Y employee in your company five and ten years from now? What skills must Gen Y master to be a leader in those positions?

_____

_____

These skills are your long-term talent development goals.

3. How many of your company's job openings were filled by existing Gen Y employees in the last 12 months?

_____

_____

You can get a strong sense of the success or failure of your talent development efforts based on how many job openings you fill internally. However, this is only true when you open a position to internal *and* external applicants and an internal applicant is determined to be the best candidate.

Having asked these three sets of questions to many groups of executives, managers, and entrepreneurs, I've identified a few areas where Gen Y needs the most help developing our professional talent. These areas for improvement are a reflection of our formal and informal education, as well as our coming-of-age priorities (Wear a tie? Come on. It's only graduation. I'm wearing a bathing suit. Really.).

I've also identified some creative ways to fast-track our learning in each of these areas so that you hold our attention and imagination (without bribing us with Starbucks gift cards). The trick is to develop Gen Y's talent while being mindful not to sound like our parents' pre-first job interview pep talk in the kitchen. Or worse, sound like an online defensive driving course. "Now watch how the 1987 blue van changes lanes without using a directional signal. What can we learn from this video?" Uh, how much we love mass transit . . .

TWO AREAS WHERE GEN Y AND YOUR COMPANY IMMEDIATELY BENEFIT FROM OUR TALENT DEVELOPMENT

- Communication
- Problem solving

It is my observation that the most effective Gen Y talent development programs *start with the end in mind* (in terms of the lessons that Gen Y should master in order to be a strategic asset) and *work backward* to connect the learning milestones with our career progress. This makes whatever you are going to teach a Gen Y employee immediately relevant to our own career and most valuable to your company's plans. This also allows you to be extremely specific with your expectations and learning outcomes. Remember, Gen Y needs a balance of immediate application and longer-term thinking to grow and deliver our best performance along the way.

Communication: Can you hit me back?

As a generation, Gen Y is infamous for sending informal (or worse, downright confusing) messages when company protocols require a formal communication. We've been told that no one is better than we are, and we believe it (just ask). We put that advice to use when we call the CEO by her first name—over the loudspeaker. We also are heavily dependent on technology for basic communication, which lends itself to a casual communication style (think serious e-mails with a powder blue floral pattern in the background and an inspiring quote about peace in the signature line). Our reliance on technology also keeps us from practicing the face-to-face communication skills necessary to work well with others in a real business environment.

Since the United States is largely a service economy, it is my belief that the fastest return on your talent development investment is to improve our communication skills in the following specific areas:

- One-on-one conversations
- Talking in front of a group
- Communicating online
- Presenting ourselves on paper
- Working with a team

One-on-one

The skills Gen Y most needs in one-on-one communication are active listening, making our point clearly, and keeping eye contact. You can begin to teach all of these to us through a simple talking point exercise. Give two Gen Yers a list of four topics we must cover in 90 seconds (which doesn't sound difficult until we are forced to start talking). These topics could be questions such as "What is your favorite movie and why?" "What is an event you clearly remember from high school?" Or a more work-related question such as, "What emerging trend or new technology is likely to impact our company next year?"

The Gen Yers should be instructed to maintain eye contact with their partners (which doesn't mean looking at the floor *together*); each person has a total of 45 seconds to make his or her points, while the other person must remember the points they just heard *without* taking notes (or hitting record on their iPod). After both participants have shared their four topics, they then repeat the most important aspects of each of their partner's answers—while continuing to hold eye contact. To take this a step further, they can then share their partner's answers with the rest of the group or with you as their manager.

Do this a few times with different talking points and your new hires will become better at staying on topic and actively listening. You can also customize this exercise to fit your standard customer interaction or other time restrictions. If you work in a service business that has a relaxed tempo, you might also challenge your Gen Y employees to talk with customers for an increasingly longer time. Start by asking them to try to talk for one minute, and then coach your employees to build up to five minutes. Experienced executives will tell you: "Small talk can lead to big sales."

To a group

Gen Y best learns public speaking in front of a live audience (and I'm not talking about Skype). To help us develop our presentation confidence and skills, ask us to research something related to our job and present a summary of our findings. Or you might ask new employees to attend a business meeting with the understanding that we will have to later share a few key points based on what we observed. Start out by asking us to present what we learned in a short period of time, maybe two to three minutes (trust me, to some Gen Yers this will seem like an eternity). Then give us larger projects with increasing presentation times and deliverables.

Every time we present in front of a group, give us feedback, starting with something we did well before discussing something we could do better. Always end with another something we did well. The capstone of this training could be the opportunity to present in front of several company executives or other business and industry leaders. Speaking to those in charge is not only good practice, but also allows us to show off our potential to the people we know can influence our career. If you have a Gen Y employee who really could benefit from better public speaking skills, suggest that he or she joins a group like Toastmasters. You can also share with him or her my six tips for better public speaking at www.ysize.com/speaking.

Online

This is Gen Y's most comfortable communication channel, and because of that it is often our most lax mode (i.e., annoying to Boomers and anyone else who can diagram a sentence). We are well-known for not completing sentences in our e-mails, ignoring *Spell Check* or *Grammar Check*, and then hitting the most dreaded button ever created: "Reply All." Feel free to post my six rules for communicating online somewhere in your office where Gen Y will see them (I suggest wherever your Wi-Fi signal is strongest):

THE GEN Y GUY'S RULES FOR ONLINE COMMUNICATION

1. *Set your e-mail (both on your computer(s) and cell phone) to automatically Spell Check and Grammar Check every outgoing message.* This will save you huge embarrassments, such as misspelling your boss's name in your e-mail *to the entire division.*

2. *Never ever send a mass e-mail without listing the addresses as BCC.* It is rude, unprofessional, and impersonal. It also shares our e-mail addresses with people we don't know and increases the recipient's chances of getting spam, viruses, and other Web nasties. Show your recipients some respect by blocking out our e-mail addresses. Otherwise, it's like signing up all your business contacts to be alerted every time one of your friends updates his or her Facebook page (if you've made this mistake, you'll know *exactly* what I'm talking about). Ding.

3. *To hit "Reply All" is to respect no one. Never use this feature unless it's an emergency* and 911 has stopped accepting your calls. In fact, Zappos gives a Dunce Cap to the person who uses "Reply All" the most. They deserve it.

4. *Be extraordinarily specific in the subject line of your e-mails.* Summarize your reason for the message, the action you need the recipient to take, and your timeframe. When you simply hit "Reply," the recipient may not know you need a fast response and instead prioritize your e-mail just above the 12 spam messages touting free all-natural weight loss supplements made with inventa-berry (which you've never heard of before because it was only recently found in the deepest corner of the Amazon desert).

5. *Don't forward personal messages and non-work related items to people at work or on their work e-mail.* I've met several people who have been fired because they forwarded inappropriate jokes, pictures, videos, or hyperlinks at work or to work colleagues. One manager told me that a promising Gen Y employee sent several photos of herself out having fun with friends to a few coworkers. No big deal, except she was dancing on the bar while *wearing* her company shirt! Remember, any e-mail sent from or to a work e-mail address is the property of the company, and they can use it against you.

6. *Do not use exclamation marks and emoticons with every sentence.* This is important!!! ☺ ☺ ☺

On paper

Even though we don't communicate on paper as much as we used to (except for occasional executives I meet who have their assistants *print* their e-mails—why?), there are at least three rules Gen Y should follow in addition to shredding and recycling our used paper:

1. *Know the proper format for your document.* This is a big deal when you are communicating with managers and executives who value protocol (and margins).
2. *Read your document out loud before sending.* You will catch the errors that *Grammar Check* and *Spell Check* missed. You will also impress the person in the cubicle next to you.
3. *Save all your best business communications in one file.* Use this as a resource so that you can save yourself time and continuously write better (or at least get more benefit from that one paper you wrote really, really well).

On a team

Good team players respect the dynamics of having to work with and rely on teammates who may think, act, or believe differently from ourselves. To teach Gen Y how to work well with others on a team, give us team-based assignments of increasing difficulty. Start us out easy by assigning us to participate on teams with people like us (that way we're all late together), and then give us more responsibility and increasingly diverse team members.

While Gen Y is known for being tolerant of diversity, that does not mean we are skilled at leading diverse teams. The biggest challenge for Gen Y is to lead a team of people of varying ages, ethnicities, education levels, and backgrounds who are working in multiple locations and who don't necessarily agree with our vision (and who think they should be the one leading the team). If we can do this, we can take on just about any team-based assignment—except for laundry.

Problem solving: Google required, # 2 pencil optional

The second area in which Gen Y often needs help to develop our talent is problem solving. How your employees solve problems can determine whether your company survives, fails, or flourishes—especially in these challenging times. Rather than simply identifying problems, you want your Gen Y employees to bring you potential solutions with each problem we discover. (Otherwise we point out the leak in the bathroom but don't think to turn off the water.) Getting Gen Y employees into the habit of solving problems on our own develops our critical thinking skills and allows you to give us increased autonomy. The best companies groom employees to view every problem as an opportunity for innovation and to see every setback as a laboratory for learning.

To make problem-solving a strength among your Gen Y employees, we must be taught how to quickly identify problems, define the range of options for solving them, choose the best plan of response, and give evidence to our supervisors as to why we think we have the correct response. (This is especially true if our boss is in Gen X and naturally skeptical of our ideas.) In other words, rather than complaining that the cash register is broken, we need to say that the cash register is broken and we've already taken two steps to get it repaired (and found a calculator so that we can make change for cash purchases in the interim). You can teach all of these in three creative *Y-Size* ways, all of which can lead to *huge* wins for your company:

1. Coach Gen Y to ask for opportunity

Gen Y eagerly wants to demonstrate our abilities and, hopefully, impress you enough to earn recognition and advancement within your company. You ignite this line of thinking by coaching us to ask for opportunity *every* day. This literally means that we go and ask a supervisor for the opportunity to solve an actual problem facing the business, streamline a business operation, research a potential product, or try to tackle any other dilemma that, if solved, would move the company ahead.

One 24-year-old receptionist at an engineering firm was coached to ask for opportunity. When she asked, her boss suggested that she complete a government Request for Proposal *for practice only*, since their company had no chance of winning. The receptionist sat at her desk and answered the phone, made coffee, and helped clients. In between these responsibilities, she finally completed the practice RFP after three weeks (now *that* is dedication!). She took it to her boss, who reviewed it with her and then suggested she mail it in to get a feeling for the entire process. When she did, he congratulated her on completing the task and said she had earned the right to work on the company's next official RFP writing team. She was very excited, because this was her first real promotion.

Six months later, in the middle of the day, her boss called an emergency all-company meeting. He announced with great fanfare that the company had just won its largest contract *ever*. The contract would double the company's revenues the following year and require them to hire a lot more people. Then he asked all the employees to thank *the receptionist* for winning the company the contract!

She was met with tremendous applause. Then the boss said, "You asked for the opportunity. You made the most of it. You are the new Project Manager." By asking for opportunity, she learned new skills, received a huge promotion, and doubled the company's revenues, all in her first year on the job. Now I would want a person *of any age* to do that for my business!

2. Designate a brainstorm wall

Gen Y wants to help management solve difficult technical problems and strategic questions facing the company or division. We also like to be creatively challenged and encouraged to "think outside the box" (although we're not too sure we're in it). You can turn these natural tendencies into a competitive advantage by creating a Brainstorm Wall. On a Brainstorm Wall, management writes specific questions they are facing, or strategic decisions they are contemplating, but have not yet been able to solve. These questions could range from how to increase market share in a specific area to finding the right work-around solution for an engineering problem.

The best Brainstorm Walls—in terms of participation—are located in high-traffic employee common areas, such as conference rooms and hallways. Employees are asked to write our best answers to the questions on the Brainstorm Wall (which can also be a designated whiteboard or flip chart) at any time and then sign our names. We can also write observations related to the question, add new pieces of data, and even ask other questions that might be helpful to answer the original question.

Creating this highly visible interactive open forum for exchanging ideas and possible solutions reinforces employee teamwork, dismantles departmental barriers, and gives all employees a voice in problem solving. In my experience, it's sometimes the people with the fewest years of service or smallest titles who think of the nontraditional answers that management is having difficulty seeing (often because these employees don't know what you can't do—they only see possibilities).

The bottom line is that a Brainstorm Wall is a simple, low-tech way to automatically multiply the number of people trying to solve your business problems. This cognitive diversity allows a company to approach one problem from many different directions, which leads to new sets of possible solutions—all of which can mean a better answer faster.

If you don't have a large wall, whiteboard, or flip chart suitable for this type of tangible idea exchange or if your business is decentralized, you can accomplish the same idea exchange by creating a secure Wiki where employees can post our solutions to your prompts online.

While every answer on a Brainstorm Wall will not be correct (although I promise some will be amusing), each answer and observation will move management closer to the right answer. In other words, the writing on the wall may be exactly what you've been looking for.

3. Make innovation the norm at your company

Innovation is courageously asking "What if . . . " and "Why not . . . " when others are saying, "Whatever." To make innovation the norm at your company, you have to encourage risk-taking and support those who take the risks—formally and informally. The companies that become market or industry leaders—and stay in that position—are the ones that encourage employees *at all levels* to take the calculated risks that can move the entire company forward. Two ways to unlock innovation are a Bright Idea Contest and a Quarterly Innovation Challenge.

In a Bright Idea Contest, employees have three minutes to pitch a panel of company executives on our best idea for a new or enhanced product, service, or other business idea. Monetary awards are given for the best Bright Ideas, and the winner of the contest can receive seed money to move to the next step with their Bright Idea. This ongoing focus on ideation leads to more ideas that can help your company grow, increases participation in the idea process throughout the company, and can reduce the time it takes to turn ideas into results.

For more ongoing innovation, launch a Quarterly Innovation Challenge. In this voluntary challenge, employees are presented with an actual problem facing the business every quarter. We try to solve the problem in 1,000 words or less, using the following framework: Demonstrate that you understand the problem; identify the resources available to solve the problem; present your strategy for solving the problem; and explain how you would measure results. If our solution gets chosen, we get recognition, a small prize (maybe money, lunch with an executive, or funding to attend our industry conference), and we are asked to provide a more in-depth solution along with playing some role in moving our idea to the next step.

If you don't want to organize or lead a larger innovation initiative, at the very least ask Gen Y for our opinion when trying to solve problems that don't seem to go away. Gen Y believes that even if we are not the smartest or most experienced persons in the room, we are, at least, as well-intentioned and therefore have a perspective that should be considered. At one manufacturing company, the plant manager was struggling with a manufacturing problem that had plagued his company for 10 years. Two young engineers asked for a chance to tackle the problem, and with the guidance of an older employee solved the problem—leading to a *$25 million* net positive impact! So go ahead and ask us what we think. We might have a solution you've been looking for—and 25 million reasons to validate how smart you were to ask us for our opinion.

READING PAYS

One final missing piece of our talent development is traditional in nature but generational in terms of consequences. It's been my observation, and it's reflected in actual sales, that Gen Y does not like to read business or professional development books. As a writer (and avid book reader) it's hard for me to understand this mindset. But I can't tell you how many times I've asked a group of Gen Yers to share with me the last work-related book they read cover to cover and seen them shrug their shoulders before responding with a Dr. Seuss title. And yes, I know that Gen Y can read; we read www.cnn.com, www.espn.com, subtitles on Adult Swim, and our favorite fashion or pop culture magazines. While these types of reading materials can be entertaining (Who doesn't want to know what happened on *Jon & Kate Plus 8*?), it's probably not the information that will help us develop our workplace talent and abilities (although they do deliver a powerful message on the challenges of multitasking).

Gen Y's lack of enthusiasm for reading work-related books (and probably most books for that matter, especially thick ones) leads to concerns from employers that we are not pushing ourselves to develop our professional skills on our own. Some employers feel this lack of ongoing professional education could become a long-term hindrance for Gen Y's development—and I agree (with the exception of those who "read" our books via audio download or on Kindle).

Employees of all ages must continually grow our knowledge base in order to stay current by expanding and challenging our previous thinking. This is especially true as competition forces organizations to continually improve if we are to survive and thrive. One solution I found for encouraging Gen Y to read is a Reading Pays program.

To implement Reading Pays, your management or senior leadership compiles a list of 50 books with messages they feel would add value to employees if we read them and acted on the key points. These books can be organized around core competencies that the company identifies (such as your company's values or strategic plans) or be based on more subjective reasoning and personal preference. The company then offers to pay employees $50 for every book we read on the Reading Pays list *if* we write a three-page report that details what we learned from the book and our plan for implementing the book's message in the workplace. We receive the $50 when we turn in an update 30 days later explaining the results of the actions we took based on the book's message.

If a Reading Pays program is too much to ask of your Gen Y employees or your company's culture, then make the information medium more *Y-Size* centric. Instead of providing a list of suggested books, offer a list of suggested podcasts, case studies, and online videos from subject matter experts (such as those on TED.com), or some other multimedia or less traditional information form. While the thought of these nontraditional education sources might make you a bit uncomfortable, this may be exactly the right strategy to keep your Gen Yers up to date.

MAP IT TO THE TOP

Once you've taken steps to develop Gen Y's workplace talent, the backbone of our continual talent development is a customized Career Map.

All Gen Y employees you want to retain should receive some sort of individualized Career Map within our first 90 days at work. This Career Map is our answer to filling in the blanks between where we are now and where we see ourselves going with our career at your company. Even if Gen Y employees say we don't want a long-term career at your company, give us something tangible that shows us on paper that a rewarding career is right in front of our nose (or adjacent to our eyebrow ring). When you provide us with a tangible map, it adds at least one more consideration to our decision-making process as we decide whether or not to stay with your company long term. Some companies, particularly those with frontline positions that have a history of high turnover, go so far as to post a Career Map on the wall. Whatever works for your culture is what you should use.

A customized Career Map always starts with an employee's current position and then walks us through the various paths for advancement within the company. When creating a Career Map, always include the achievements or outcomes and specific skills required for each position on the map, as well as any necessary certifications, technical or language proficiencies, and advanced degrees an employee must master to claim that position (and no, winning at Wii Bowling is *not* a certification). You don't have to re-create this type of job-related information; it's the same info you use for posting the job opening for that particular position. By providing this level of detail, you can show Gen Y each and every step between where we are now and our dream job at your company. In the process, we should realize that there are many different career paths available to us within the organization and that we can adjust our path based on our life experiences and changing priorities (such as the start of a new college football season). Most importantly, we need to see that no matter where we are in your company, there is *always* a path to the top.

How important is a Career Map? I've interviewed numerous Gen Y employees who tell me they've left companies because they were unsure of the steps between their current job and their dream job within the company. This makes sense, because Gen Y wants to know that we are on the right track and consistently making progress. If we don't know the specific steps involved in reaching our career goal at your company, we can't tell if we are making progress. Instead, we may feel as if we are spinning our wheels—even if we aren't. Many in Gen Y would rather quit a job than feel like we are stuck moving our mouse in circles in our beige-carpeted cubicle.

One of the most motivated Gen Y employees I've ever interviewed told me that he works so hard because he knows that every day he is moving closer to his goal of becoming a bank branch manager. He knows this because his current branch manager has showed him on paper each step in the path from teller to branch manager. While I was talking with him he recited each and every step ahead of him in his career *without using notes.* This 25-year-old employee explained all of this to me with great pride and enthusiasm—and his boss wasn't even in the room! Then he explained which step he was on and how soon he expected to reach his goal. He made it clear to me that knowing the steps involved in his career path made him work harder, because he could see he was making progress every single day. Now that is talent you can bank on!

Y-SIZE QUESTIONS

1. What does your current talent development program look like? Can you tell if it is effective based on your rate of internal promotions?
2. How does your company foster creativity, innovation, and risk-taking among employees of all ages and experiences?
3. Do you provide employees with a Career Map or something similar? Could you?

CHAPTER 11

Professionalism Is More than Bling

(It's about making the cash register ring ring.)

Vegas, baby, as in, "What happens in Vegas stays in . . . ." It's one of those storied towns where adventures are to be had but never divulged. Unfortunately, that's rarely the case any more. Thanks to camera phones, YouTube, and worst of all, Twitter, our worst errors in judgment can live forever online. A good Gen Y friend of mine, who shall remain nameless, was invited to attend a major industry trade show with his real estate company in the casino-rich city. This was his big opportunity to impress his boss and schmooze current and potential customers. He was determined to make a name for himself among his colleagues—*and, boy, did he*. On the first day he worked his trade show booth like a pro, attended a few instructional seminars, and then geared himself up for the famous post-trade-show parties.

To keep up with his older colleagues, he started drinking at the first Happy Hour and kept toasting and drinking until he had so much to drink that he got sick—right in front of his boss *and their clients!* He spent the rest of the trade show apologizing (and nursing an awful hangover). The impression he made was certainly unforgettable, but not in the way he intended. He also ruined a nice pair of leather shoes.

Unfortunately, this story is not one-of-a-kind or limited to Las Vegas. I've seen some of the smartest, most highly degreed young professionals make unbelievable rookie mistakes when it comes to professionalism in the workplace. The reason is simple: They lacked the experience to make better choices. Sure, many of them *knew* better, but that wasn't enough for them to *choose* better. The hard truth is that *professionalism is a 100 percent learned skill.* Rather than having us learn it the hard way (what I call the Vegas way), you can shortcut our learning curve by teaching us some cornerstones of workplace professionalism so that we best represent *you* (on and off camera).

Professionalism in the workplace has never been more important for companies than it is now for one basic reason: Customers have choices, and they know it. The more choices they have, the more they can expect in return. This is particularly true in businesses where Gen Y is the public face of the company, the first and last person a customer (or client, or patient) encounters. In these companies, Gen Yers are the receptionists, servers, and hosts, as well as nurses, engineers, lawyers, accountants, and other professionals early in our careers. We are what customers remember (Marge, where is that comment card?!).

DEVELOP PROFESSIONALISM AS A PART OF WORKPLACE TALENT

Most managers with whom I visit know that Gen Y can use some polishing when it comes to professionalism. Unfortunately, the closest many of us in Gen Y get to in-the-trenches training on workplace professionalism is watching a marathon of *Celebrity Apprentice* (but Joan Rivers does have something to teach all of us). Our need for training on how to act like a professional directly dovetails with the upside potential of developing our workplace talent. By combining the two, you get a Gen Y employee who *thinks* like a professional and *acts* the part. (Plus we don't ruin our nice shoes.)

The frustration caused by Gen Y's lack of professionalism boils over when we do things that seem so painfully unprofessional to other generations that they can't believe we actually did them. (This would include turning up the volume on our iPod *while* our boss is reprimanding us for listening to it at work.) Worst of all, sometimes Gen Yers don't even realize we've done something wrong. You can see this in action when you give us seemingly clear instructions such as, "Answer the phone like a professional," and then we answer the next phone call with a mellow, "What up?"

How can that not be professional? That's what the mega-rich celebs do on MTV's *Cribs*, and surely they are professional. They have two assistants and a poodle in their purse (just the poodle, not the assistants). I mean, even the CEO of Facebook started out with two business cards. One read "CEO"; the other read, "I'M CEO . . . BITCH." (And, no, I'm not making that up. It's as eye-opening to type as I'm sure it is to receive.)

TEACH GEN Y THE PROFESSIONAL EXPERIENCE TO DELIVER

The challenge is that broad terms such as "good customer service" or "act like a professional" can mean something very different to Gen Y than to other generations. For example, Boomers expect that when they make a purchase using cash, their change will be counted back to them. Gen Y thinks this whole "counting-back-money thing" is an absolute waste of time. I remember standing in line at a coffee shop when the Boomer in front of me asked the Gen Y cashier why he didn't count back his change. The Gen Yer said with complete sincerity, "Why? You can't count it?" I almost fell over. The cashier wasn't trying to be rude; he just had no idea this was what he was expected to do. To make your Gen Y customer interactions as professional as possible, employers should *repeatedly* practice and refine the experience they want Gen Y employees to deliver.

One potentially compounding factor in teaching Gen Y professionalism is that many managers I interview assume Gen Y employees will not be around for long, so why train us? With a little *Y-Sizing*, however, you can teach Gen Y how to act like professionals in less than 30 minutes, and with only a few simple steps. Start by identifying which areas of professionalism most benefit Gen Y (I've identified some for you) and how to teach each of them to us (which I've also included for you). Once you provide us with this training, you have every right to hold us accountable to a higher standard of professionalism.

FOUR PILLARS OF PROFESSIONALISM:

1. Dress for the job you want (not necessarily for the job you have)

Give your Gen Y employees actual photos of how we should dress if we want to be taken seriously by our colleagues, bosses, and customers. If you want to mix it up, give us samples of different clothing options and let us tell you which are acceptable (dress slacks), which aren't (seeing our silk heart boxers because our dress slacks are three sizes too big), and why (because it's a law firm, silly!). Along with these photos, list your top five *extremely specific* rules for dressing like a professional, such as no flashy jewelry, minimum skirt lengths, hair color and piercing options, and even the types of shoes allowed. One practical lesson I always share when speaking to young professionals: You dress for the part you get. If you want to be taken seriously in business, then dress as if you mean business.

Keep in mind that whatever guidelines you give us regarding attire must be consistently enforced; otherwise you (and the guidelines) lose all credibility. And for those who think I'm ruining a person's individuality by suggesting that our employer limit our hair colors or clothing styles at work, please know that I personally think blue hair and baggy pants are cool. So are pink hair and an eyebrow ring. But if your company's customers don't like it (meaning they go somewhere else), then it's time to rise to their expectations. It's our customers, not our boss, who make our jobs possible. So spike your hair on Friday evening at 6 PM, and part your hair on Monday morning at 6 AM. It's what I do . . .

2. Who you know determines how far you go

After you've made Gen Y's day by giving us our own business cards
(yay!) and tactfully suggesting we wear a different type of less-
see-through shirt (not yay!), then send the message that our business cards have little value unless they are in someone else's hands.
To make this happen, I recommend that you have a regular contest
in which your Gen Y employees are challenged to hand out a certain number of business cards in person or make a certain number
of professional contacts online through services such as LinkedIn. By
asking Gen Y to keep track of how many contacts and connections
we make, we are able to monitor our progress. And so are you—
especially if you keep track on a big whiteboard we can all see in the
office. This also reinforces the idea that *every* day we can meet someone new who can help us, and our company, move forward.

3. Check your professional image online

Whenever I make new business contacts, I immediately look them
up on the Web (often on my phone before I even get back to my
office). And I'm not alone. Sometimes I'm shocked by what I find
online with little effort, and the person I just met should be shocked,
too! It's my belief that Gen Y, especially given our reliance on the
Internet, should Google our first and last names *every* week. This
only takes a second (actually it takes less than a second, and Google
will tell you so), and the results are powerful. I also advise Gen Y
professionals to sign up for Google News Alerts so that we are notified whenever our name pops up on the Web. This service is free and
super easy to use. If your Gen Y employees find things on the Web
that don't cast us in a professional light (you know what I'm talking about), either suggest we try to remove the unflattering material (especially given the camera angle), or play defense by writing a
bunch of well-written blog posts and signing them all with our full
name so that they push down the other search results.

4. Ethics are what you do when no
one is looking

Gen Y has come of age in a time of major ethical lapses. We've
seen Enron implode (I remember going there for a recruiting tour

in college!), Madoff bilk billions from investors and charities, and numerous other people concoct all variety of scams and deceits. (Apparently I've got $20 million in my name being held by the Nigerian government. So, apparently, do you.)

To help Gen Y decipher the difference between what's right, what's wrong, and what feels right but is still wrong, give us some basic guidance on how to make ethical decisions. This could be as straightforward as advising us to consider decisions from different perspectives: What would Mom and Dad say if they found out? What would strangers say if they found out? Who might get hurt from this decision, and do they know that is a possibility? The simple act of stepping back from a decision and considering multiple perspectives before making a choice can help lead a Gen Yer toward the best decision (rather than what seems like youthful fun at that moment). You can also ask us to consider our decision from varying timeline perspectives, such as how big a deal this would be in five days, five months, and five years.

PRACTICE MAKES PROFESSIONAL

To make sure your training sticks with Gen Y, have us role-play the work experiences you want to create. The easiest way to do this is to ask one Gen Yer to role-play a customer and let a coworker pretend to sell them something, solve their problem, or handle their complaint in a professional manner. Then, have the two employees reverse their roles. I've found role-playing to be *extremely* effective for teaching professionalism to Gen Y because we are so geared to learn by doing (and because we enjoy stepping into the shoes of the upset customer who just trashed us *and* mispronounced our name).

One manager shared with me a story about teaching professionalism that really hit home. He told me that he had a Gen Y employee who was having trouble creating the customer experience that their company was famous for delivering. The manager told him, "You've got to create the experience that you had when you first came in here as a customer." The Gen Y employee responded with a shrug, saying "My first experience here was applying for a job."

The response stopped the manager in mid-sentence. Until that moment, he had never considered that maybe the employee had not shopped at their particular store before applying for a job. After all, many Gen Yers went to work at this particular company solely for the product discounts. Because this employee had never actually shopped in the store, he was unable to understand the customer's point of view. No wonder he couldn't create the experience—*he'd never had it!* The manager gave the employee a gift card and told him to come in unannounced one day and experience the company from the other side of the counter. After that one shopping experience, the employee finally understood what the manager was talking about and was able to replicate it.

Another way to reinforce professionalism is to have a manager or company trainer shop each employee every few weeks. In this process, the manager waits in line along with other customers. When it's his or her turn, the manager asks all the questions a typical customer might ask an employee and rates the employee's responses. Then, the manager goes into more off-the-wall questions about order customization, making special requests, and things related to the company's mission, values, or history ("So, the paint looks pretty new. When was this company founded?").

The employee is scored on his or her greeting, product knowledge, and interpersonal skills, right in front of the other customers. At the same time, the person asking the questions obtains an accurate snapshot of the employee's professionalism, which they can then track in future shopping experiences. I've seen this technique in action several times and am always amazed by the interaction and outcomes. Not only do employees learn and have their learning reinforced every few weeks, but the experience also keeps all the nearby coworkers on their brightly colored toes, too.

MAKE PROFESSIONALISM S.O.P. (STANDARD OPERATING PROCEDURE)

Another way to approach professionalism is to go ahead and make it standard in your operations. For example, at one of the fastest growing haircutting franchises in the United States, every stylist must shake each customer's hand *before* starting their haircut. Now that's a different start to a $14 haircut! Nordstrom's also takes this approach, but at the end of the sale. Once a customer (such as myself) has paid (and I've uncrossed my fingers, since it seems the credit card worked), the salesperson comes out from behind the counter to give the customer his or her bags personally and to thank them for shopping at Nordstrom's.

In keeping with company policy, the salesperson doesn't sling the bags over the counter or rush you off; instead, he or she takes those two extra seconds to walk around the counter and make the end of your buying experience personal and exceptional. These small employee-to-customer interactions reflect your company's professionalism and showcase that your people are true to your brand.

SECRET SHOP TO GET THE INSIDE SCOOP

Competition is fierce, but just how fierce? It's one thing to say the competition is tough, but the best way to prove it is for your Gen Y employees to experience it firsthand. You can give us a front-row seat to evaluate the competition when you send us to secret shop a competitor known for operational quality or excellent customer service. To secret shop the competition, give an employee a list of three to five major things to observe in our secret shopping experience. We are to compare these three to five major things to the experience our own company provides and evaluate what is and is not working in our company's favor—and what we could do about it.

If we work at a restaurant, we can go to a competitor for lunch. If we work at a retailer, we can go shopping at our competitor in the afternoon. If we're selling insurance, we can call our competitor and ask for a free consultation by phone. Most companies can find a way to let Gen Y sample the company's biggest competition in a respectful manner (and leave knowing just how much better we have to be to compete).

When secret shopping the competition, I do hold fast to one rule: If you're going to look, be sure to buy. This is only courtesy. I've also found that most salespeople are *way* more forthcoming than they should be about their company when you buy something, so buy something small, strike up a conversation, and use it as a learning experience for your Gen Y employees (revealing all the things you shouldn't tell your competition when they are secret shopping you!).

RISING STARS, MEET YOUR FUTURE AT COMPANY MEETINGS

Few things represent as strong a display of a manager's support for a Gen Y employee as inviting us to an important company meeting or outside-the-office business event. Attending these meetings—even with limited Gen Y participation (i.e., "sit here and take notes")—is viewed as a major vote of confidence in our future (and a crash course on how to act really interested when we have no idea what the person across from us is talking about). The ideal type of meeting to which you might take your Gen Y employees is a quarterly management meeting or retreat, a major industry trade show, or a high-profile community leadership event (such as a fundraiser or awards banquet). Smaller local events, such as a Rotary or a Chamber of Commerce meeting, also are good steps in fostering Gen Y's emotional connection to you and your company, steps that allow us to check out a different type of professional environment (preferably one with an open bar).

To help your Gen Y employees make the most of these experiences, meet with us beforehand and suggest the three or four most important actions or interactions that we should pay particular attention to during the event. These could be instructions to observe how the meeting is conducted, how people introduce themselves to each other, or what the primary topic of conversation among the attendees is. (Notice that it often has nothing to do with work.) Also give us a heads-up as to appropriate dress. If possible, send us an advance copy of the event itinerary (or a link to one on the Web), and explain what we can and cannot do in terms of participation. (No, the open bar is off limits to you, greenhorn.) Earning an invitation to these meetings, especially within our first few years of employment, sends the message loud and clear that we are being groomed for bigger opportunities within the company. So invite us to attend and let us make you proud (that, or act like you don't know us when we interrupt the CEO in mid-speech).

LIKE, PROFESSIONALS HAVE TO TALK, YA KNOW, LIKE PROFESSIONALS

After taking the employee to the event, ask us what we saw that was expected and what was different. Help us to identify one or two areas we can focus on to better prepare for these types of meetings in the future. Simply listening to the conversations that take place at these events creates valuable exposure and emphasizes the type of communication skills we will need to succeed (such as, like, saying sentences without using "like," like every other word, ya know?).

One of the best implementations of this strategy I have collected was used by a large government organization. They instructed their managers and leaders to take one rising star to each quarterly meeting. Being selected to go with your boss to these quarterly meetings became a big deal, worth way more than a favorable employee review, and employees worked hard to earn a coveted spot. If your company does not have a quarterly or annual management meeting, you can reward employees by taking us to an industry event (such as taking us to market in the apparel industry) or allowing us to go to a vendor demonstration (such as in the manufacturing industry). Taking a rising star to a meeting builds our confidence, teaches us valuable skills, and publicly connects our future with your company. (Plus we get all those cool free samples that make us popular with our friends.)

If you want to tie this back to on-the-job skill mastery, ask us to make a brief presentation at the meeting, write a report about major lessons learned at the event, or instruct us to share our learning with colleagues who couldn't attend (but tell us not to rub it in, at least not too much). Experience is a great teacher of professionalism. Create situations where Gen Y has to be a professional, and we will rise to the opportunity.

PROFESSIONALS JOIN UP

Almost every occupation and industry has a nonprofit organization or trade group that offers professional development, camaraderie, and exchange of best practices that will be immensely valuable to Gen Y throughout our career (as well as to our employers). However, Gen Y is not taking advantage of these associations. I don't blame us for this one, though. Many associations are only now realizing that they can't just mail us a brochure promoting a topic we've never heard of and a "hot lunch buffet" with a room full of strangers 20 years older than we are (how welcoming!), and expect us to show up en masse. Adding weight to this dilemma is that many Gen Yers don't automatically value industry designations, so that we don't see that the more industry designations we earn, the better prepared we will be for career advancement.

The truth is that joining a professional or industry association not only develops our professionalism but also keeps us up to date on the trends in our career field. Furthermore, it helps us see our job in the context of an entire industry. (Who knew there were 20,000 graphic designers—let alone in one convention hall?) Whether we join a local, state, or national association, the point is to meet, learn from, and grow with others in our profession.

The bonus for employers is that a Gen Y employee who becomes active in an industry or professional association becomes an automatic *recruiting tool* for your company. If you can't convince your Gen Yers to consider joining an association, at least suggest we sign up for our industry or occupation's news alerts and free publications. This steady stream of work-related information will not only help keep us more current, but once we find out that the national convention is going to be held in a warm location, we'll want to join ASAP (especially if you're paying!). For a sample list of major industry and professional associations, visit www.ysize.com/ch11.

If your Gen Y employees are still uncomfortable with joining a professional association, we can find some level of work-related connectivity and learning by joining web-based discussion groups specific to an industry or occupation on sites like Facebook or LinkedIn. These groups might be professional networks, discussion boards, or other collections of people with a shared interest in a topic, industry, or occupation, and they usually have some type of moderator or sponsoring person. However, don't be fooled into thinking that just because a discussion group is labeled "fleet maintenance" that we're discussing work. Go ahead and join the conversation and see if we're talking about hydraulics or hip hop.

To truly *Y-Size* our participation in professional associations, nominate Gen Y employees for association awards. Receiving one of these awards is a big deal for Gen Y and makes your company look very good. We will invite our parents and friends, and Twitter the entire time we're at the event (including while we're receiving the award on stage). Simply being selected as a finalist will make us feel good and let us know that you value our hard work and potential. If one of your Gen Y employees wins one of these awards, promote it in the media, on your company web site, and in your company or industry newsletter.

LEADERSHIP: "FOLLOW YOU *WHERE*?"

Leadership is a difficult skill to teach but a critical one to learn if we're going to be professionals. When I interview Gen Y, we often have many different definitions of leadership, but we all can point to one or two people we consider a leader. This is a great starting place for teaching us about leadership. Ask your Gen Y employees who we consider leaders and why (and they must be real people, no cartoons or Harry Potter characters). Then ask us to explain what makes the "why" so important or meaningful to us. Ask us to list two or three times we have been forced to lead, and what worked for us, what didn't go as expected, and what we would now do differently (who knew someone could lead a coup against you in a nonprofit organization?!). With that in mind, it's time to officially make us *Manager for a Day*.

"MANAGER FOR A DAY" PROGRAMS BUILD TALENT

In this *Y-Size* action, you bridge the gap between what Gen Y thinks leadership is all about and what leaders in your company actually do on a day-to-day basis (and no, it's not play solitaire on their computer, that's just a rumor). Remember, your Gen Y employee may have taken five leadership classes in high school or college but may have never actually been responsible for leading five people in a work environment, let alone five people who think we are too young to be leading them.

In a Manager for a Day program, a Gen Y employee—who has reached some tenure or performance goal—takes on the responsibilities of an actual manager for one full workday. This hands-on exposure gives Gen Y a more accurate view into the world of management, highlights skills we need to develop to eventually become a manager, and enables us to better communicate with management by creating a shared frame of reference.

THE BEST MANAGER FOR A DAY PROGRAMS

The best Manager for a Day programs give Gen Y employees an assignment the night before, which sets up at least one goal for the program day. When the employee arrives, there is a list of items that need his or her attention (ideally the same list the manager uses every day, or the one you created to look even busier than normal). The Manager for a Day must deal with the items on this list while handling the typical daily management responsibilities, such as resolving customer issues, handling employee requests, and communicating with different divisions and vendors. Depending on the level of management the employee is assuming, it may be necessary to have an actual manager shadowing the employee (especially when an upset customer doesn't like "Because I told you so" as an answer).

There are two ideal times to provide constructive feedback about our professionalism during the Manager for a Day program. The first is at lunch, when the manager shadowing us can highlight specific actions we should focus on for the second half of the day (like catching our breath). The second is at the end-of-the-day debriefing (when we're in shock that we only finished half the list and never made it to the bathroom). Ask us what part of the job was similar to what we expected, what was different, and what the biggest lessons we learned were (mainly that being a manager is harder than it looks). Also let us know what areas you think we should work on as an employee to develop our management skills. Any feedback you give should be constructive and immediately actionable—in the best case, actions we can adopt the very same week.

Many Gen Y employees participate in a Manager for a Day program without knowing whether or not going into management is one of their goals. But they always come away from the experience with a new level of respect for the manager. At a minimum, the Manager for a Day program gives Gen Y a more accurate perspective into management (such as why you need a land line when the power goes out), which will help both management and employees in future communications. At a maximum, this program can ignite a passion for advancing our career with your company that we did not have before.

"MANAGER FOR A DAY" CAN CREATE MANAGERS

This happened for one young professional, Denise. She became an Administrator for a Day at her organization five years into her career. On her day there was a major crisis resulting in emergency response crews. She was the point person for two hours until the actual administrator returned. She had to deal with the media, employees, and high emotions on all sides, which made her realize that she had what it took to become an administrator, something she had never considered before. With coaching and encouragement from her boss, she became an administrator the very next year. Denise said that never would have happened had she not tried out the position for one day.

If it's not possible for your Gen Y employees to become Manager for a Day for legal or other reasons (no, you can't go into the snake pit by yourself), then create an event where we are challenged to solve typical management situations via role-play. The situations could include coaching an employee who shows up chronically late to work, responding to a nearby competitor lowering its prices, celebrating an employee landing his or her largest sale ever, or helping an employee to communicate better with coworkers. Add specific details (and even back stories) to these different situations to make them more realistic. (A stand-in photo of a competitor can add authenticity—and a coloring surface.)

Then ask your employees to attempt to solve the problems in each scenario—either individually or in groups. Many of these scenarios have more than one answer. Your goal is not to assess us based on finding the right answer but to walk us through the decision-making process, which will help us to think and act like managers (so that you can actually take a lunch break).

LEADERSHIP DEVELOPMENT PROGRAMS

For larger companies that have the resources, motivation, and vision to develop their next generation of talent at a deeper level, the best option is to create a Leadership Development Program (LDP). I've spoken at these programs—and have many friends who've participated in them—and I've always found them to be a tremendous advantage for Gen Y participants and their employers. Not only are these programs a boon for recruiting talented Gen Yers, but they also take your best and brightest employees and push us to grow incredibly fast. In addition, an LDP gives the employer excellent insight into participants' professional potential.

A typical LDP (sometimes referred to as a Rotational Development Program) starts with applicants who are high-potential current employees or new hires who have recently finished college or graduate programs. These applicants are rigorously screened, interviewed, and tested. Only the very best gain acceptance into these programs. The more selective the program, the more prestigious our acceptance appears inside and outside of the company. (Some managers call it the LDP halo effect). An LDP usually kicks off with more testing and group trials, such as personality assessments or problem-solving quizzes, after which the participants begin intensive teambuilding and workplace training for a short period of time.

Each participant is then assigned to work in a specific division or area of the company for a set time period (usually eight months). The LDP participants start at a higher level than comparable new hires and feel *much* more pressure to perform. The pressure comes from higher stated expectations, as well as from being tracked by the employee's manager or LDP program leader. Often, progress reports are given to company executives, too.

The LDP participants also get together a few times each year to undergo more intensive training, problem solving, executive briefings, and role-playing. After the first eight-month assignment, the employees are reassigned to a different division, often in a different geographic location. The stress of moving to an entirely new place and having to start all new work relationships pushes participants to grow and adapt—and they might move three times in two years!

LDP CAN BE BUSINESS BOOT CAMP

In some ways, this is much like a boot camp for the business world. The regular LDP communication and meetings continue, and then after another eight months participants rotate jobs yet again. Once the LDP is complete (they often consist of three rotations in about two years), a graduation is held and attended by the most senior leadership in the company (and, of course, by our parents). Upon graduation, the LDP participants are given the option of several positions within the company and then placed on an accelerated management track.

I remember speaking at one LDP graduation in the Northeast. The event was very fancy and high-energy, and you could tell that the Gen Y employees in attendance had big futures (and they weren't shy about reinforcing that belief). But the highlight was when the chairman of the company, which has over 70,000 employees, gave a talk on where he thought the company was going and then took *unscripted* questions from the LDP participants. It was an incredible experience.

If your company wants the benefits of a Leadership Development Program but doesn't have the resources or desire to create one from scratch, consider joining a local training consortium or working with your area colleges to partner on developing an intensive training program for emerging professionals. You might also consider offering a series of advanced training options off-site as a reward for high-potential employees who meet tenure or performance goals. Either way, teaching professionalism will definitely help your Gen Yers to put our best foot forward—and pull up our pants. Now that is a win/win, especially if you're walking behind us.

Y-SIZE QUESTIONS

1. Does your company offer some type of professionalism training for employees?
2. Do you encourage Gen Y employees to become active in industry and professional associations, seminars, and conferences?
3. Could your company benefit from a Leadership Development Program?

CHAPTER 12

Motivate Gen Y by NOT Giving Us a Trophy

(Or, "Keep your gift card. Can I leave work 30 minutes early on Friday?")

I remember walking into the 200-year-old cathedral and looking straight up at the ornate ceiling. I had never seen anything like it. Before I could take in all the history, the pulsating boom of music and techno lighting stole my attention. Then a singer took the stage, and then another one followed. Soon there was so much energy filling the room that it was hard not to get motivated—and that was exactly the point. Then Steve Fleming, executive vice president of sales for Ceridian Canada, a human resource solutions company that processes more than 4.7 million Canadian pay statements a month, took center stage to really kick things off.

For the next two hours I was awed by the best employee awards show I've ever seen, and I've seen *a lot* of them in my speaking and consulting. Rather than the requisite "Here's your plaque" (name to be engraved later) and "Now let's take an uncomfortable posed photo in front of everyone while we sweat profusely in the bright lights," each award winner was introduced with a funny build-up from Steve. Then a photomontage of the award winner was broadcast on big hanging screens for everyone to see. The photos showed each winner with his or her family, on different non-work pursuits, and having fun at work. In short, everything was personal.

This was my favorite part: A voice would project over the speakers, and it would be a recording *from the award winner's family* calling to congratulate them on winning their award! The recordings were heartfelt, inspiring, and hilarious. My favorite was a son whose congratulatory message went, "Dad, I'm so proud of you. I can't believe you actually won something!" I almost fell out of my chair with laughter (and so did everyone else). However, that fall was completed when they showed a picture of an award-winner's first car, which made the term "road hazard" look like a compliment. It also underscored how far he'd come with the company. Everyone in the audience was clapping and hollering and celebrating. Simply amazing—and that's before the dancing began!

THE BEST AWARDS PROGRAMS INSPIRE ALL FOUR GENERATIONS

This awards ceremony stands out because it was the first one I've attended that inspired all four generations in attendance—including Gen Y. Ceridian Canada did this with the personalized (and funny) award-winner introductions, candid photos of employees at work and play (big with Gen Y), specific sales numbers for the top award winners (which resulted in a universal "wow" from the audience), and hilarious audio recordings from parents, spouses, and children. *And* they did all this in an unconventional setting—the 200-year-old cathedral—along with music and entertainment that was universally appealing.

After sitting through so many boring awards ceremonies (where you could tell the executive handing out the awards didn't know what he was going to say ahead of time). I can't begin to tell you what a breath of fresh air it was to attend this event and see colleagues cheering when someone hit a sales milestone. Most impressive was that one person produced the entire award event, the same event that had taken three people to produce the previous year. The one person was a 28-year-old Gen Yer named Aileen, who deserves her own award (and a recorded message from her mom)!

THE BEST GEN Y MOTIVATION IS PERSONAL

While a blowout event in a 200-year-old cathedral might not fit your company's culture, pocketbook, or PR strategy (thanks, AIG!), there are myriad ways you can motivate employees to higher performance without breaking the bank (thanks, too, CitiBank). While the specific tactics you employ will differ based on your company's traditions, size, industry, and even governmental regulation, a conversation about employee motivation always proves *highly personal*. Learning what inspires a human of any age to pick up a phone and make their 42nd cold call in a row (after being rudely rejected the 41 previous times—six of which were in a different language) reveals something deeply authentic and vulnerable about what drives them. The same goes for motivating employees to continuously perform better when doing the minimum alone will earn them job security.

My research shows that *employee motivation is a combination of logic, emotion, and current life priorities*. The logic comes from wanting to create an outcome that has a tangible or intrinsic value, such as earning a paycheck so that you can keep your house. The emotion comes from the pursuit of the goal (and the inherent risk of failure), the ups and downs that add suspense along the way, and the feeling of achieving your goal (especially if they announce it alongside a photomontage). Both the logical and emotional aspects of motivation are strongly dependent on an employee's current life priorities as well as our underlying beliefs and values. It stands to reason that these priorities will change over time as we accumulate more life experiences (i.e., get older), as people start counting on us outside of work (such as children or aging parents), and as varying situations cause us to challenge our priorities (maybe we lose our job or an event like 9/11 pushes us to take a new look at what we do with our time). In essence, employee motivation is basically Maslow's Hierarchy in action at work.

The *Y-Size* insight is recognizing that the top of the hierarchy can look different to different generations, especially Gen Y. Sure, people of all ages might be motivated by some type of recognition or reward (and also want to avoid things like pain and hunger). However, we also tend to have a preference on how we want to receive that recognition or reward for it to be most meaningful.

MOTIVATE GEN Y BY GIVING US WHAT WE *REALLY* WANT *(THE BEST PART: IT WILL LIKELY SAVE YOU MONEY!)*

If motivation is basic human nature, why are executives, managers, and business leaders telling me they struggle to consistently motivate Gen Y employees? They tell me that the standard gift cards and Employee of the Month nameplates are not working as well or at all. In venting their frustration, these business leaders reveal a motivational truth that I've seen again and again in the business world: *People tend to try and motivate others based on what they find personally motivating.* This, too, is human nature.

We assume, particularly when we're busy and successful, that people want similar things to what we want—after all, it gets us out of bed at 6 AM on a Saturday (must be a Boomer). At the same time, these types of motivational tools are easy for business leaders to give because they are comfortable and safe (plus they can get the plaques in bulk). The problem is that what Gen Y wants and needs to be motivated to put forth our best effort is often different, and in some cases *very* different, from what our bosses in other generations are enthusiastically dangling as an oversized carrot. This is frustrating to our bosses when they don't get the results they want; it's also deflating to the Gen Yer who feels his or her boss is out of touch when he or she excitedly rewards us with a brand-new VCR.

THE BEST MOTIVATORS CAN BE CHEAP AND EASY

The irony *and opportunity* is that what Gen Y actually wants is often much cheaper and easier to give than what our bosses are enthusiastically waving around (and where do you buy a new VCR anyway?).

This has everything to do with Gen Y valuing lifestyle and relation-ships above work (which means we view time as a currency), as well as our current life stage (mid-teens to early 30s). In comparison to Generation X and older generations, we presently have fewer depend-ents (not including our unemployed roommates) and fewer long-term responsibilities than those older than we are.

Additionally, we've been told over and over, "You're only young once, so make the most of it!" Our priorities are simply different *for the time being.* Eventually we will probably gravitate toward the same types of incentives that other generations prefer. But that won't be until we "grow up" (or until our parents cut us off and our room-mates skip town without paying rent).

The *Y-Size* advantage for the immediate future: Discover what your Gen Y employees actually want and how we want you to give it to us. Then you remove the guesswork about getting the results you want in less time and with less effort (because you're not wast-ing either one). You also might discover that what we want is less expensive than what you used to offer, especially if what you're cur-rently offering is not getting the results you need.

So, how do you find out what Gen Y wants in order to show up to work early, give it our best, and maybe even stay late once in a while? Ask us. We *want* to tell you.

MOTIVATE GEN Y IN WAYS WE TRULY VALUE

I know that asking Gen Y what we want to be more motivated at work could seem like opening Pandora's box and adding a double espresso. However, my experience interviewing Gen Y says this is not the case. Gen Y may seem a bit unrealistic in what we think we *deserve* (like a promotion after one month), but we have a reason for wanting it (we did show up *most* of the time).

For example, I've found that Boomers tend to motivate others based on the external trappings of success. These are the things that they find personally motivating, such as plaques, applause, and—most of all—cold hard cash. My research shows that while these tangi-ble displays of achievement have a certain value to Gen Y (espe-cially if the applause is from our friends during Happy Hour), they don't have nearly the value to us that Boomers place on them. While Boomers might work late into the night to earn a $50 bonus, Gen Yers might be much more motivated to work through our lunch break if we could earn the right to leave work 30 minutes early on Friday. Heck, we might even show up a minute or two early on Monday!

PROVIDE MOTIVATION THAT DRIVES THE PERFORMANCE YOU WANT

The irony and *opportunity* for you as a business leader is embracing the idea that giving a Gen Yer 30 minutes off work might be less costly to the company than the financial bonus you were planning to offer (especially since we stop working at 4 PM on Friday anyway). At the same time, if your tried-and-true motivational strategies are not working as well any more, then it's time to consider trying something new. Different generations simply have different motivational hot buttons, and it's time to adjust your offerings so that you consistently drive the performance you need.

I know that the very idea of replacing your Employee of the Month plaque ceremony may seem risky, but I promise that when you invest a tiny amount of effort to learn what your Gen Y employees actually find motivating, your efforts will be much more effective right away. You also won't have to hear the Gen Y joke: "Employee of the Month. Means you're a winner *and a loser.*" Not only will you likely save money and get better results with less effort, you will also show you are a better steward of your company's resources. A side benefit is that once you're motivating us in a way we value, we will want to be measured for the results we create. (Yes! Now where is that Excel spreadsheet . . . ?)

We may even provide you with the mother lode competitive differentiator: discretionary effort. This is when Gen Y employees are so committed to achieving an outcome that we do more than the minimum to make it happen. Hallelujah! It's like us not simply putting the dirty dishes in the break room sink, but actually rinsing them and putting them in the break room dishwasher. (If you've ever been in an employee break room with a kitchen sink, you know precisely what I'm talking about. And no, for the record, those dishes weren't mine. The JRD initials scribbled in my handwriting on the bottom are a mere coincidence. But can I have them back?)

ASK AND YE SHALL MOTIVATE

When you take a few minutes to learn what motivates your Gen Y employees, you not only show us that you are a leader attuned to our needs, but also that you value us as individuals. This individual consideration by itself is often motivating to Gen Y. What you find out may also surprise you with its simplicity (I'd really like to get a new laser mouse for my computer) or become a starting point for a creative way you can at least move the Gen Yer toward a variation of what we want. (No, I can't give you a Ferrari, but I could offer you a subscription to a Ferrari magazine.) At one company they found the most motivating reward for their Gen Y employees was not gift certificates but having their boss personally wash their car if they met their big goal. This "white collar car wash" not only worked to motivate the employees, but it also gave their boss a chance to prove his word was good—and that he was in on the fun. (Alas, they also learned he wasn't very skilled at washing cars.)

If you don't ask Gen Y what we find motivational, you also risk doing more harm than good. Gen Y can be very turned off by one-size-fits-all motivational tools (such as the standard-issue poster of an eagle hanging in the office that says something like "If the wind is in your face, turn around"). We see prepackaged inspirational gestures as insincere. They also reinforce the stereotype that our employer is out of touch (especially if the poster wasn't printed on recycled paper).

The same caveat applies to you proudly giving a performance reward featuring a $100 gift basket full of gourmet smoked sausages, not realizing after five years of continuous employment that the Gen Y recipient is a vegetarian. I've seen this type of no-fit reward happen several times at different recognition ceremonies, and I never know who to be more embarrassed for: the five-year employee who just realized how out of touch the boss was with her, or the boss who just realized how out of touch he was with the employee (no wonder she didn't eat any hamburgers at the company BBQ).

START WITH A LIST OF OPTIONS

To save yourself (and the award winner) from the embarrassment of a well-intentioned gift gone wrong, all you need to do is *ask* Gen Y what we want to be motivated. This is easy to do in a way that takes little time and that fits your management style. I recommend that you create a list of potential rewards or incentives you're willing to offer and let us rate them based on how motivating we find them.

You can then sort our individual rankings in different ways to fit your specific goals. You can group them based on what an entire division finds most motivating to create a division-wide incentive. You can also use them to find the best way to motivate different employees at the same level within your company, such as frontline managers. The rankings can be sorted based on typical responsibilities or even by geography. (For example, offering a camouflaged hunting jacket and matching duck call as an incentive does not get nearly the oohs and ahhs in San Francisco that it does in Oklahoma City—I've seen people in Oklahoma City get really excited about this gift set!). By documenting and aggregating the top answers for the employees you lead, you've created a flexible, customizable resource that you can rely on to effectively motivate both individual employees and specific groups of employees.

Some possible motivational rewards:

- Unpaid time off from work in varying increments. This could be leaving work early on Friday, extending our lunch break by 30 minutes, or the big one: earning a full unpaid day off from work. This is particularly good when you are trying to reduce costs but still want to reward employees for performance by giving us a lifestyle reward.
- Let us select our next project, role, or problem to solve. Yes, this is actually motivating. We want to prove ourselves. Give us the chance and you could get a double win.
- Arrange lunch or coffee with a senior leader. Hint: make sure the leader pays and is told ahead of time how to pronounce our name correctly.

- Try new technology first. This could be a new company cell phone, GPS, or software configuration.
- Spa treatment. Ah, bubbles. Now that is the Gen Y lifestyle! Rubber ducky not included.
- Host a small party for the office at 5 PM with a budget of $50. Can you say grass skirts for everyone?
- Tickets for sporting, entertainment, or community events. These are most memorable if we can bring a friend or our family and have preferential seating or access. Be sure to consider nontraditional events such as motocross and fashion shows.
- The old standby: gift certificates. Gen Y prefers gift certificates for cool local stores and restaurants. If you can't give those, then the best gift certificates offer lots of options for use (such as ones through a credit card company). Make sure you always include a personal note along with the gift certificate. The note should explain why we are receiving the gift certificate and your enthusiasm for us earning it.
- $50 to spend on improving our office or cubicle. Somebody's gotta get rid of that shag carpet.
- A financial bonus. If you choose to give money, make sure to include a handwritten note. A personalized message from you is what adds meaning and emotion to the moolah. The message should also reinforce the outcome that led to the reward.
- Give us your parking spot for a week. It's okay; you'll remember why it's so great, and we'll never forget.
- Donation to a nonprofit of our choice. This can be a triple win: motivate your Gen Y employee, help a great organization, and get a tax deduction.
- Fantasy car rental for a weekend or a limo for a night.

At Emplicity, a professional employer organization based in California, their Employee of the Month gets more than a good parking spot. They get free use of a Mercedes or Prius for the entire month! Now *that* is rolling in style. Jennifer Meehan, a 24-year-old employee at Emplicity, agrees: "At first the idea of driving the boss' car was intimidating, but now it's exciting to think that for 30 days I can replace my old Civic with a Mercedes, or better yet, a Prius with carpool lane access! This definitely isn't the type of company that my parents worked at in their 20s." Still don't believe me? Check out pictures of the Emplicity cars at www.ysize.com/ch12.

MOTIVATION BY THE NUMBERS

Once you have a list of what motivates specific employees as well as entire employee groups, you then tie this motivational mix to a clearly defined and *mutually* agreed-upon metric. Keep in mind that your employees will focus their efforts on whatever area or outcome you choose to measure. This could range from customer service reviews and manufacturing quality to sales volume and shipping efficiency. I've found with Gen Y, it's smart to tie a reward or incentive to both our individual job performance and some team-based metric. This allows Gen Y to shine as individuals (which we want to do), and also sends the message that we must work as a team for the big payoff (we sometimes need to be reminded of that one). Whatever type of reward you offer, be sure to base it on *above average performance*. This will remind Gen Y (and your other employees) that doing a "good job" is not good enough for them or the company to reach their goals.

CREATE A TIMELINE FOR REWARDS AND PROVIDE THE CLOCK

Once you've agreed to an outcome and how it will be measured, the second part is to create a timeline that meets Gen Y's criteria. It is my personal observation that *short-term incentives should only be used for role clarification*, such as opening new accounts in a specific week or month. Short-term incentives are all about reinforcing specific actions, outcomes, and risk-taking in the immediate future. *Long-term incentives, however, should be tied to an increased value in the company and sustained performance.*

How short is short-term? I recommend that Gen Y employees have a goal we are striving for every month. This is short enough to keep us focused, but long enough so that we can see whether or not we are making progress. Combining these short-term goals in sequence should put a Gen Y employee on track to meet our long-term goals.

When it comes to long-term goals, meaning those more than six months out, I must add a Gen Y word of caution: When you focus your motivational metrics on long-term goals, such as annual goals, you are going *way* beyond the timeline that is customary, comfortable, and reasonable for most Gen Yers. Unless you break an annual goal into smaller goals—quarterly, monthly, or something else— we simply will not be motivated to take immediate action to reach the goal. Why? Because we don't feel any sense of urgency. The timeline is just too disconnected from where we are presently to where you are trying to get us to focus in the future.

While long-term goals with extraordinary payoffs can come in handy for retention, keep in mind that retention alone does not mean better performance. In other words, if it were a marathon and we were at the starting line, help us to focus on completing Mile 1 on time rather than worrying about finishing the last mile strong. Trust me, when we get to that last mile, we will know exactly how close we are to the payoff (and post-race celebration!).

Once Gen Y is on the path to giving our top effort, it's time to give the best of the best what we deserve: recognition in front of those we care about. You can think of this type of meaningful recognition as the way people on the sidelines of a marathon cheer runners to the finish line (or in Austin, the way bands play along the marathon route—really). Recognition in front of those we care about doesn't put a dollar in our pocket, but it can make all the difference in whether or not we find that inner fuel that propels us forward when the going inevitably gets tough.

RECOGNITION: IT'S LIKE LOOKING GREAT AT YOUR 20-YEAR HIGH SCHOOL REUNION

It's no secret that Gen Y likes recognition (just ask my little sister; she has her own "Honor Wall" in my Mom's house. Not that I've noticed . . .). Frankly, Gen Y tends to like any attention that highlights something positive about us. The one aspect of recognition that is often misunderstood when it comes to Gen Y is that *bigger is not necessarily better*. For Gen Y, it's much more than who is recognizing us, it's actually *who knows that we've been recognized*. The right type of recognition—in front of the right group of people—can be a powerful, cost-effective form of motivation that you can use over and over again.

To make recognition meaningful and most effective, it must be sincere, specific, and credibly brought to the attention of the people we want to impress. It's important to note that I'm specifically using "recognition" instead of "praise." There is much commentary in the media that Gen Y is simply praise-hungry. Sure, we like praise (who doesn't?), but when it comes to motivating us at work, I think too much praise is a bad thing. It increases our feeling of entitlement, often bringing with it diminishing returns. When you praise too often you also risk sounding insincere, which is a major turnoff. Instead, I believe in recognizing Gen Y when we've *earned* the recognition, not because we simply showed up to work on time four days in a row. We should show up on time. It's our job. That's what we're paid to do.

There are three different ways I've found to recognize Gen Y for little or no cost and to achieve maximum impact. I'll start with my absolute favorite.

CATCH US WORKING—AND TELL SOMEONE WHO CARES

The coolest recognition I've ever seen for Gen Y employees I learned from an administrator at a large school who was trying to motivate everyone, not just Gen Y. He wanted to recognize his entire staff for their hard work, but he wasn't able to offer them any traditional rewards such as a cash bonus, profit sharing, gift cards, or a salary increase. Instead he thought of something ingenious (from a Gen Y perspective).

He borrowed the school's digital camera and took an action photo of every single employee, from the custodians to the school counselors, doing their jobs. These were candid photos of the cafeteria workers preparing food, teachers teaching, and the maintenance crew conducting repairs. Right before the winter break, the administrator printed his favorite action photo of every employee and put it in a thank you card.

Then he wrote a handwritten note to each employee's *parents*, thanking them for raising a child who now helps so many children. He then sent the cards, with each employee's action picture enclosed, *without telling the employees.* If he couldn't find their parents, he would send the card to a spouse, sibling, grandparent, or even their old college dean—someone who would make an emotional impact when they unexpectedly called the employee to say that they had received a thank you card, complete with action photo, for the role they played. The administrator told me that when he returned to his school for the first day after the holiday break, his employees were hugging each other and sharing stories about the calls they received. He said one newer Gen Y teacher seemed more emotional than the others, so he asked her if it was the note he wrote in the card. He said he made it very specific to her and all she gave to the school. She replied with tears, "No, it was the photo. My mom had never seen me working."

If you want to do something similar and your company does not have a holiday break, consider sending the cards or some other personalized correspondence right before a holiday when Gen Y employees will likely be with our families, such as Thanksgiving. I promise it will be the talk of the meal (and make Grandma proud).

OTHER MEANINGFUL WAYS TO RECOGNIZE EMPLOYEES

If notifying an employee's family or other close friend is outside your comfort zone (or legal boundaries), there are many other ways you can effectively recognize a Gen Y employee within your company. You can recognize us on your company's homepage (good press for everyone and an easy link to our blog), Intranet, newsletter, e-newsletter, or employee or customer magazine. You can also have the CEO, another executive, or even our direct supervisor interview us for their monthly podcast (if you don't have one, you should).

You can even create a tradition where you spontaneously hand out some type of symbolic reward that recognizes an employee for exhibiting the best of what your company is about. This could be something that ties in with your company's business, such as a vintage company T-shirt (very cool!), or your core values, such as a goodie bag filled with Earth-friendly stuff. The more unexpected the things in the goodie bag, the more memorable (such as a regifted ribbon for first place in bowling in 1982). Who wouldn't want to brag to their friends about receiving that?!

ACKNOWLEDGE EXCEPTIONAL EFFORT

When an employee, particularly a Gen Yer, does something truly exceptional, I believe you should go public with your pride in us. You do this by recognizing us in the media. If an employee helps you secure a patent, call local reporters and explain why the patent is so important, and how it could help with future business growth and economic development. If your employee receives community acknowledgment or a civic award, submit a press release to your local newspaper, trade publication, or business journal. These positive media features—even if they only make the newspaper's web site—lead to unexpected feel-good phone calls and e-mails from people with whom we've lost touch, as well as congratulatory messages from family members, friends, and former classmates.

Be sure to also notify the media of any extraordinary acts of service undertaken by your Gen Y employees outside of work—such as the Gen Yer who performed CPR on a stranger and saved a life, or the one who opened his or her apartment to those less fortunate. You may even consider creating an "Employees in the News" section on your company web site where you highlight our successes and achievements along with links to the press release or media coverage.

Whenever your employees' successes are featured in a newspaper, magazine, trade newsletter, or online, send a copy of the article along with a congratulatory note to the employee, our spouse, and, if possible, our parents or family members. You might even consider sending a copy of the article to the employee's alma mater for inclusion in our alumni update and posting in our career services office. Rest assured that if your Gen Y employees are featured in the news, we will forward the media link to all our contacts, Facebook friends, and online groups. These media mentions make the Gen Y employee feel good and simultaneously showcase why your company is a great place to work (plus they get us to read the newspaper!). This also attracts more Gen Yers to your company because we seek out companies where our peers are getting ahead.

A WELCOME VISIT FROM THE POLICE

A police lieutenant told me how he unexpectedly motivated a young Gen Y police officer to peak performance—without increasing his salary or giving him a promotion. The lieutenant was on a routine drive that took him past the young officer's parents' house. On a whim he decided to stop in and talk with the parents. He said he wanted to let them know what a great job their son was doing.

To the lieutenant's complete surprise, the young officer was at the house visiting with his parents (and, no, he wasn't supposed to be working). Rather than talk to the parents in private, the lieutenant took the opportunity to tell the young officer's dad—in front of the officer—that he should be proud of his son for the excellent work he is doing. The lieutenant said you could have heard a pin drop when he recognized the young officer in front of his dad. He also said that literally overnight the officer became one of the best in his entire department, and it was all because he took five minutes to say the right thing in front of the right people.

If you're not getting the response you need from your motivational efforts, find out what will work and make a change. Not only will you be more effective with your resources, but we'll be more excited to receive the gift. (After all, the free car wash isn't that exciting when you don't have a car. Can you wash my scooter?)

Y-SIZE QUESTIONS

1. What outcome would you most like to motivate your Gen Y employees to create?
2. What is your primary strategy for motivating employees?
3. Have you asked your Gen Y employees which incentives they find most motivating?

CHAPTER 13

Retain Gen Y —and Our Enthusiasm

(Or, Gen Y doesn't quit. We just stop showing up.)

In my speeches I often joke about my generation's uncanny ability to quit a job when we no longer feel it's a fit. Sometimes we give notice (usually when we have another paycheck coming), and sometimes we don't (because we still owe you money for the uniform). At some point an executive or manager always seems to chime in, "Jason, I don't believe Gen Y would just up and quit." And then it happens to them. Stefan, a financial services executive, had this exact realization, about which he e-mailed me after hearing my presentation at an event for successful entrepreneurs.

> I work at a large, very traditional, highly stuffy investment management firm. Everyone wears suits and ties; there are nice views

from all the offices, and expensive art hangs on the walls. It's fair to say that the movie *Wall Street* is an accurate portrayal.

This past Tuesday and Wednesday, I was out of the office all day for meetings. I tried several times to reach my Gen Y assistant, to no avail. Not talking to her for a full day is highly unusual, but two days in a row is unheard of—I mean, her earpiece seems permanently attached.

When I returned to work on Thursday morning, the other Gen Yer on my team came into my office. She carefully closed the door and whispered, "I have to talk to you." She told me that on Tuesday morning my assistant had been working as usual, and then at about 10 AM she picked up her handbag, put on her coat, and walked out of the office. The staff thought she was simply going for coffee, as she often did. *But she never came back.* Instead she e-mailed the office manager from home later that day to inform him that she was ceasing her employment with us.

I was so shocked that I called her cell phone, and after leaving two messages explaining that I wasn't upset, she finally called me back. I asked her what happened. Why would she just quit without any notice or explanation?

"I just wasn't feeling it," she said.

What does that mean? Who quits a job in the middle of the day because "you're just not feeling it?" But that was her entire explanation. Then she told me she had already chosen a new direction: She had just booked a trip to Mexico. For three months.

If you've ever had a valuable employee quit without warning (and possibly without telling you), then you know how frustrated Stefan felt. One day you're counting on the employee, the next day he or she seems to have dropped off the map (or taken off to Mexico, which is about the same thing). While the *Y-Size* process detailed in this book is designed to attract, engage, motivate, and develop Gen Y employees, the real payoff comes when we perform for your company at a higher level *over a longer period of time.*

RETENTION IS A DOLLARS AND SENSE ISSUE

It's simple economics that employees are overpaid when we are first hired (because you're paying us to learn how to do the job), with the intention that at some point we will generate more value than you're paying us (at least that's the goal on paper). This means that for you to really earn the benefit from having Gen Y employees, you need us to increase our value as quickly as possible and then stick around as long as possible. You achieve this increased retention by moving us from the attitude of having *a* job to an attitude of having *the* job. It's this type of employment attitude that increases our average tenure *and* keeps us from going across the street for a latte and ending up on the beach with a margarita.

In fact, each additional day you keep a high-performing Gen Y employee, you increase the return on your employment investment. You directly reduce turnover costs, which can average anywhere from 150 percent of the employee's salary to *several times their salary* if they're in a high-demand or high-skill position. The indirect savings can be even more valuable: continuous operational quality, sustained customer service, and reduced disruption for management and colleagues (because they don't have to take over our job in addition to theirs). But first, you must become fluent in what your current retention story is saying about your business in order to write a better *and longer* ending.

TENURE CYCLES I: AVERAGE TENURE TELLS YOU PART OF THE STORY

When companies try to measure their effectiveness by employee retention, the most common indicator they use is tenure, or how long an employee has been continuously employed by their company (which, by the way, has only minimal correlation to an employee giving top performance during that time). Tenure is easy to measure, and it matches the Boomer and Mature definition of loyalty, which is based on months and years and, in some cases, decades. Gen Y measures loyalty a little differently—by placing an emphasis not on how long we worked somewhere, but on *how hard* we worked during the time we were employed. This is why Gen Y can quit a job after three months and, with all sincerity, ask you for a job reference. Sure, we only stayed three months, but "we worked *really* hard the *entire* time."

When it comes to retention, many executives are now focusing more attention on retaining quality employees rather than on retaining all employees, because retaining talent is a competitive advantage by itself. This is especially true in highly skilled businesses with an ongoing workforce shortage, traditional businesses that are on the verge of a massive retirement bubble, and service businesses with historically high turnover (i.e., they need new employees for every shift).

To improve your Gen Y retention (both for top performers and those simply saving you from doing the dishes yourself), start with a candid look at your current retention data. The key is to be *candid*, otherwise you can easily bias your data to show you want you want to see (or, more likely, what the person giving you the data wants you to see).

The first step is to determine the average tenure for all employees. If you have a large or highly bureaucratic company with an aging workforce (think: government and old-line businesses) this number can be easily skewed toward those with longevity, which is why this data is interesting, but not necessarily useful.

The more important number, at least in light of this book's goals, is to determine the average tenure of your Gen Y employees (those born between 1977 and 1995). This tenure will not be as long as your overall employees unless your company is brand new, because Gen Y has not been in the workforce that long. However, this should still give you plenty of valuable data to work with when determining how to increase Gen Y's retention.

TENURE CYCLES II: WAYS TO INCREASE THE VALUE OF YOUR TENURE DATA

• If possible, eliminate from your data the employees fired for cause. You want to focus on keeping the employees who are adding value, not the ones stealing your rolls of toilet paper. Employees fired for cause are not a retention issue but a hiring issue.

- What are the tenure points (broken into three-month periods) when Gen Y is most likely to leave your company? Do we tend to leave after one month, six months, 18 months, and so on?
- Do we leave at a particular level or job responsibility within your company? Is this new, or is it a problem common to your business model or industry?
- What other patterns can you see from the retention numbers? Do certain bosses (or franchisees or geographic regions) have lower retention numbers? Do Gen Y employees leave at a certain time of year (not including seasonal hires)? Do employees who complete orientation or required training stay longer?
- What other data do you have about why employees leave? Are you more successful retaining Gen Y women than you are retaining Gen Y men? Can you distinguish between employees who had no choice to leave (such as those who had to follow a spouse who was transferred to a different state) from those who went across the street to work for your competition (and took three of your best customers with them)?

TENURE CYCLES III: MAKE THE NUMBERS TALK

To figure out what your tenure cycles are saying about your business, look for patterns within the questions you just answered. These patterns will show you where to focus your retention efforts. Pay special attention to people leaving at certain positions or during certain months, and look to see if certain bosses have abnormally high turnover compared to their peers (which will be obvious when they are compared side-by-side).

To fine-tune your review, ask these same questions but limit the data to the tenure cycles of your top-performing Gen Y employees. Keeping low performers is okay (after all, they don't want to leave), but keeping the best of the best is your real goal. You want Gen Y to stay at your company not because no one else wants us but because we see your company as the best fit for our talent and future.

I've seen the power of this connection on display at companies where Gen Y has taken a pay *cut* to help our employers weather this difficult economy (or rejected offers from competitors who dangled more money). From a Gen Y viewpoint, this short-term financial sacrifice is a long-term investment in the company and its mission and leadership, as well as our future. (It also lets us bank lots of good-will for when we ask for Friday off). This kind of deep employer-employee connection comes from turning an increase in our average tenure into actual Gen Y loyalty, which will be discussed in detail in the next chapter.

The simple act of organizing, revising, and reviewing your retention trends can highlight important patterns that might otherwise get lost or overlooked in the aggregated data. Sometimes the message is so obvious you won't believe you didn't see it sooner.

One executive in the car business told me that he had missed a big retention issue right under his nose because he was only looking at the data from an overall tenure perspective. He said his overall retention rate was not as good as he would have liked, but that there was not an obvious pattern he could identify.

When he finally looked at the data from a more detailed perspective, in this case separating out the month employees actually quit, he instantly noticed a disturbing trend. Gen Y employees were leaving in big numbers during the same month, but since they had different start dates he hadn't noticed this trend before (because their average length of tenure varied). It didn't help that he was five levels and four states away from this particular group of front line employees, otherwise he probably would have seen the trend much sooner.

Why would these employees leave at almost exactly the same time? The pay wasn't different, and the company mission and management hadn't changed. To find out what was going on, he called one of the recently departed Gen Y employees and asked why he left the company. The answer: The weather turned cold, and the employee didn't realize he'd have to work outside. The employee said he and his Gen Y coworkers who quit would rather work somewhere else for the same money if it was indoors or heated, which is what they ended up doing. The next day the executive had space heaters installed where the employees stood outside. Problem solved.

AN EXIT INTERVIEW IS THE MISSING LINK TO RETENTION

In my experience, employees leave a job for a reason (or several). Sometimes we quit because our boss is difficult; sometimes we quit because we no longer like what the company stands for; and sometimes we quit because our new work schedule conflicts with our sleep patterns (it really is hard to start every day at 10 AM sharp). There is never "no reason" why we quit; you just have to be more inventive to find out our true motivation for leaving.

While many experts hold fast to the idea that employees almost always quit a boss rather than a company, I believe that what a company stands for can go a long way toward keeping a top performer in spite of a jerk boss (just watch *The Office* and you'll see what I mean). No matter your personal belief on why employees leave, one thing is for sure: You've got to find out *why* employees leave *your* company, especially when your best employees bow out gracefully and take the HOV lane directly to your competition (along with a mental copy of your customer list).

The missing link to deciphering why your employees leave is an effective exit interview, which also happens to be the most under-utilized retention tool at most companies. If an employee's first day at work is their most important day to them, then their last day at work can be their most important day to you and your company. As critically important as exit interviews can be, I've found that many bosses simply choose not to conduct them. They seem to avoid them in the same way as an employee who quits without notice sends a friend to pick up their final paycheck.

Here are some reasons why. Bosses who don't conduct exit interviews fall into one of three categories:

- They simply don't care why an employee left ("Don't let the door hit your a*s on the way out"), and instead want to focus on hiring the next person.
- They don't want to hear that the employee's leaving is somehow their fault.
- They assume they know why an employee is leaving, and they like their assumption.

Don't fall into one of these traps! Gen Y employees quit for a reason. Sometimes our reasons are valid (going back to college), and sometimes our reasons are ridiculous (going back to college to study underwater basket weaving *for the third time*). But either way, identifying the "why" behind our walking out will help you to better hire, retain, motivate, and develop your most important Gen Y employees—your existing ones.

ASK THE RIGHT QUESTIONS IN YOUR EXIT INTERVIEWS

An exit interview is your chance to get direct insight into the mindset of an employee who has found a reason good enough for him or her to justify parting ways with your business. At worst, you may hear some things you don't like or don't agree with, but at best you may gain a new perspective concerning something you could easily remedy within your organization. (And you might as well get some value from all that training you put the employee through.)

The *Y-Size* secret is to ask the right questions in the right environment to get truthful answers. Then you can decide whether or not to act on the information because *you're still the boss.* This is especially important if the Gen Y employee who quit was a top performer, was well-liked by now former coworkers, or occupied a position of authority within your organization. You will need to fill this position, so go ahead and get all the insight you can before you invest in a replacement.

While your exit interview may not convince a top performer to stay, you will likely learn some information that could keep other top performers from leaving. You'll also get a chance to leave the door open in case the high-performing employee finds out that the grass truly isn't greener somewhere else (it only looks that way in their employment brochure). This happens frequently with Gen Y employees who don't have much work experience and think working somewhere else has to be better. Many times we are straight up wrong. Should you choose to take us back, these boomerang Gen Y employees can become your most loyal and vocal company cheerleaders—because they actually understand how good they have it working for you.

TO *Y-SIZE* YOUR EXIT INTERVIEW:

- *Always try to conduct the exit interview in person.*
  Don't hire a third-party service to conduct your exit interview by telephone. On the surface, this can make the exit interview seem more objective, or at least less personal or uncomfortable; however, these are the exact reasons the data is less valuable. Some of the most important communication you will get from your former employee will be nonverbal (such as them rolling their eyes as they make up a fake story as to why they are leaving). You have absolutely no ability to notice this if the exit interview has been conducted over the phone and then transcribed. You also benefit from having some sort of credibility, perceived or real, with the former employee (such as reminding them of the time you loaned them your car to go on a date with your daughter).
- *Start the conversation with praise* for the work the employee provided, assuming you are not terminating them for cause.
- *Tell the employee the purpose of your conversation up front.*
  You don't have to call it an exit interview; in fact, I recommend you don't. Simply tell us that you want a 10-minute wrap-up conversation because as a departing employee we have a perspective you'd like to hear before we transition out. Remind us that everything we share with you is confidential.
- *Then ask us these questions in this order:*
  1. Belinda, I'm sorry to lose you, but I know these things happen. When you started working with us, you seemed excited to be a part of our organization. After __ (months/years)___, why have you chosen to leave now?
  2. Was working for our company what you expected or different than your original expectations? If so, how?
  3. If you were in my position, what is something you would do differently to keep employees like yourself here?
  4. Is there any training that you think future employees should undergo or have access to that would help them be more successful at our company?
  5. Is there a question that I'm not asking about why you're leaving that I should be asking?

- *Some alternative questions include:*
  1. Is there an experience or two that stands out as to why you feel like we are no longer a fit for you?
  2. How can we help new hires have more accurate expectations and be better prepared to succeed in our company?
  3. What do you think is the most important characteristic we should look for in future job applicants?

TAKE NOTES DURING THE EXIT INTERVIEW

Always write down the answers to our exit interview questions. This shows us that you care about what we have to say, maintains a record of the conversation, and, most importantly, keeps you from cutting us off mid-sentence when we say something you completely disagree with (which will happen, but if you start playing offense, we stop talking). Your goal is to listen and not feel the need, although you will feel the impulse, to make a case for whatever past actions they dredge up.

In an exit interview you are no longer our boss but an investigator looking for clues that could help you uncover bigger ongoing issues. Store these notes in a secure file and review them as you complete additional exit interviews. Notice if there are any trends, and, if so, figure out the cause of these trends. Employees quit for a reason. The sooner you find out if it's a good reason, the sooner you can take steps to reverse the trend (or hope the door hits them in their non-dress-code-compliant pants on the way out).

For example, one hotel general manager shared with me that he had recently lost a promising employee who had moved up quickly in his hotel. He was confused why such a hard-working employee would leave with barely any warning, especially after three great years with the company. The general manager arranged an informal one-on-one exit interview with the employee. At first the employee gave the generic "I'm looking for more opportunity elsewhere" answer. The GM knew there had to be something more, so he kept probing until he uncovered the real reason the employee was leaving: His supervisor would not give him the only day off he had requested during the entire year, his birthday.

The employee had never been late to work and never called in sick, but he wanted his birthday off to visit friends and family. He followed protocol to ask for the day off well in advance, but his immediate supervisor did not approve it, despite knowing how rarely the employee asked for time off. Rather than miss the time with his friends and family, and probably insulted by the company's inflexibility given his solid track record, the employee gave his resignation on the spot. Instead of losing a great employee for one day in the middle of the week, the hotel was unable to fill his important position for six full weeks! This exit interview not only gave the general manager insight into the different priorities of his employees but also into an area where he needed to develop the supervisor's skills.

RETAINING GEN Y STARTS WITH A LOGICAL AND EMOTIONAL CONNECTION

Now that you know why people are leaving your company, let's focus on what you can do to make us want to stay. Gen Y employees are searching for both a logical and emotional connection in order to stay with an employer long-term (i.e., it makes sense for us to stay, and we like what the company is about). One of the best places I've found to start building this type of meaningful connection with Gen Y is by highlighting *internal promotions*. These types of promotions offer both a logical and emotional connection—and send the message that you believe in your employees and your talent development process.

Equally important, you dispel the myth that the fastest way for us to advance our career is to go somewhere else (because going somewhere else presents a lot of unknowns, and we know for sure that the person across from us just got promoted—we might be next!).

Internal promotions provide internal motivation

Making a big deal of internal promotions, especially if the employee is in Gen Y, shows other Gen Y employees that working for your company is not a dead end job but a practical track to a promising career. To *Y-Size* internal promotions, you must spread the word in a way that is valuable to the promoted Gen Y employee *and* catches the attention, and possibly a little envy, from our coworker peers. I personally recommend sharing the big news with the Gen Y employee in private first (especially since we may do a spontaneous dance or cheer). The ideal situation is one where a Gen Yer's boss and his boss's boss tell the employee together that he or she has been promoted *and why*. This makes the promotion personally meaningful and gives you the ability to explain to the employee the actions and outcomes that moved them ahead.

Once the employee has been notified, call a meeting to inform the rest of the staff or make the announcement during a regularly scheduled staff meeting. Either way, let the Gen Y employee know ahead of time so that he or she can be prepared for the inevitable questions that always follow (my favorite: "Did they say anything about me?"). If your organization is too large or decentralized to have an all-hands meeting, make the announcement via an e-mail or through a traditional outlet such as the company newsletter. The critical elements to always include are the exact reasons why the employee earned the promotion. This answers the annoying but important "Why did she get promoted and I didn't?" question ("Well, first off, she doesn't corner me in the break room to ask whiny, annoying, self-evident questions . . . ").

By clarifying the reasons for our advancement, you allow other Gen Y employees to identify where to place their energy if they want to get promoted. For example, in your company newsletter, you might feature a current photo of the newly promoted employee at work (not a staged photo) along with his or her new title and responsibilities, length of tenure, the position where he or she started (an accompanying photo from that position is always a plus), and a quote from a supervisor detailing why he or she was promoted.

Internal promotions are important: make them a big deal

Announcing internal promotions also earns the promoted employee valuable recognition from our coworkers (and many toasts during Happy Hour—although we now have to pay for everyone's drinks, since we're officially "assistant store director"). One high-ranking manager in the media industry shared how she had recently given an important promotion to a young professional. This promotion came with a cash bonus, increased salary, and fancy new title. The executive made the promotion announcement to the employee during a closed-door management meeting. The employee was initially thrilled but later in the week seemed deflated rather than inspired. The manager asked why he looked so glum, given the exciting developments.

The Gen Y employee's response: "No one believes I was promoted." Because the manager made the promotion announcement during a closed-door management meeting, the young professional's peers had not heard that he had been promoted. The customary e-mail announcement from the executive had not been sent, and the news was simply not spreading. Small wonder no one believed he'd been promoted. The executive apologized for the oversight and quickly sent the e-mail. That afternoon she watched through her office window as employee after employee stopped by the newly promoted young professional's cubicle to congratulate him on his big promotion. She realized at that moment that the recognition he received from his peers was as meaningful to him as the promotion itself.

When the promotion is a particularly big one, I recommend nominating the Gen Yer for some type of community, career, or industry recognition. Receiving one of these recognitions, such as being listed as one of the "40 Under 40 Top Real Estate Agents" or "Best Young Lawyers," is a big deal for Gen Y. We will tell our parents and friends, post it on our classmates.com page (and yes, it's bragging when we put it in ALL CAPS), and even use it to help us land new customers. Simply being selected as a finalist will make us feel good, knowing that you recognize our potential and want other people to see it, too.

If one of your Gen Y employees wins one of these recognitions, promote it in the media, on your company web site, and in your company newsletter or industry magazine. Also submit all major Gen Y promotions within your company for mention in your local On the Move or business newspaper section. You can also buy an ad in your local newspaper featuring a photo of all the employees who have earned promotions at your company this year. This photo makes your company look like *the* place to work for people who are serious about moving ahead with their careers.

BUILDING LOYALTY/BUILDING TENURE

While my Gen Y friends will not like what I'm about to advocate, my interviews make me a big believer in deferred incentives, rewards, and compensation. Tying some type of bonus to a specific tenure objective is an easy way to extend how long we stay with your company. In addition to the benefit of having us around longer (and recovering more value from your initial training investment), you also get *a longer period of time to build our loyalty.* This is particularly important when you have talented Gen Yers who are not getting promoted for whatever reason (such as a hiring freeze or Boomers refusing to retire). The added tenure-based incentive keeps us excited about sticking around *and gives us more time to learn from those experienced Boomers.*

1. Deferred incentives defer turnover

When creating a tenure-based incentive, the first step is to set tenure milestones for high performers beyond the typical departure cycle—and to tell us far in advance. For me, this usually means offering a deferred bonus or reward if we stay with your company at least six months longer than usual. You can figure out what "usual" means at your company by reviewing the average tenure for someone in our current position.

As you've probably seen, sometimes it's just getting us to stay through that first season when things are super slow—or unbelievably hectic—for us to appreciate the bigger opportunity you offer and to make the transition from thinking we have *a* job to thinking we have *the* job. This is often the case when you observe one big initial flood of departures from your company (say eight months after being hired), and then the next big wave of resignations doesn't occur for three years. This tells you that if you can get new Gen Y employees to stay past their first eight months, they are likely to stay much longer.

2. Give more than money to retain Gen Y

The second step is to offer more than money as incentives. You might offer stock and a one-week vacation to a locale that aligns with your company mission. Or you could offer a monetary bonus and the ability to choose our next work location or assignment. You might even offer to pay for some type of expensive training or graduate school if we meet certain tenure objectives—and commit to new ones.

Regardless, if all you have to offer is money, then Gen Y will know that's how you value our contribution. This is not the retention position you want to be in, because if the Gen Yer is a top performer, someone else can and likely will offer us more money. Don't put you or your company in that defensive situation. What Gen Y wants in order to stay might be as simple as a bigger title, a long weekend—or picking our own desk chair.

One executive told me that his firm, which is heavily reliant on Gen Y, was moving to a new building. He wanted to excite employees about the move (especially since it was across town), so he gave them each a budget and the responsibility to select and purchase his or her own desk chair. It turned out to be one of the best retention steps he ever took—even though that wasn't his intention. Although it may sound absurd, apparently when you sit 40 plus hours per week in the same chair, getting to choose your own butt rest is a major bonus. In fact, when one employee had to resign because her husband had been relocated, she offered to buy the chair from the company!

3. Stretch Projects . . . stretch tenure

Gen Y likes (okay, loves) to be challenged at work. We also want to know there are more of these experiences around the corner if we keep showing up on time. You can push both of these retention hot buttons by giving Gen Y short-term projects and work assignments, what I call Stretch Projects, beyond our normal work responsibilities. These projects and assignments could last a few hours, a day, or longer, depending on the outcomes you want us to create (and how eager you think we are to stretch). By offering us Stretch Projects, you keep work interesting, sharpen our skills, and help managers identify our strengths and weaknesses. You also keep us from feeling like we've got nothing to look forward to at work, which is exactly the moment when we start surfing the mobile Web looking for a new job.

Stretch Projects could include researching customer buying habits to identify potential new products and services, organizing and running a quarterly management meeting, or creating a social media strategy. Other projects could involve evaluating the best places for your company's next location, investigating five ways the company can save money next week, or creating a new marketing campaign, logo, or slogan. If you can't find a Stretch Project for each of your Gen Y employees, put us on a team and ask us to work together on one larger project.

We could do this in-person or over the Web, using collaboration and project management tools such as Basecamp (www.basecamphq .com). Instruct the employees to accept specific roles, submit progress reports, and work together to deliver the final demo or presentation. The best Stretch Projects pose a challenge, expand and enhance an employee's skills (such as public speaking, research, or problem solving), and have a specific, tangible outcome that an employee can show our friends and family. Among many in Gen Y, the greatest reward for a Stretch Project well done is the opportunity to lead a bigger, more high-profile project—and to pick our own team.

4. Creative scheduling keeps creative people

Some companies have the ability to give their Gen Y employees workplace scheduling options such as telecommuting, 4-10s (four ten-hour shifts in one week, so that we get Fridays off), or arriving early on Fridays to leave early on Fridays. If your company can offer any of these scheduling options, heavily promote them to your Gen Y employees. These options allow Gen Y to meet our workplace ambitions and our lifestyle priorities, which will keep us happily at your company for much longer (and make us more likely to be on time the four days we do show up).

If your company cannot offer this type of scheduling flexibility, you might consider accommodating Gen Y's scheduling requests based on our individual track record of service to your company. For example, if we want to leave early, ask us to make up the missed hours the following week. While this can be a short-term inconvenience to you, it may be much less painful than losing the employee altogether (and all because we wanted to see *Transformers II* on opening night).

Above all, remember that Gen Y places an extreme value on our time. If given the choice, many of us would rather have Fridays off and make slightly less money than get paid overtime to work on

Saturday. This is why I recommend that you consider accommodating our scheduling requests as long as they are reasonable. If they're not reasonable, then tell us so. If they are reasonable, then find a compromise. If you accommodate our requests, we have *much* more incentive to accommodate yours (including the unmentionable: staying at work after 6 PM on a Thursday).

At one design firm, the principal, who is in Generation X, offers his designers unlimited overtime and unlimited unpaid time off. You might think that his all Gen Y design team would be running up big overtime hours (earning time and a half) in a mad dash toward early retirement. Nope. In fact, just the opposite happened. His best designer (who is *very* Gen Y) worked 82 percent of the time and billed 75 percent of her time—a *huge* return on his hiring investment—and both the Gen Y designer and firm principal were thrilled with the arrangement.

You, too, can take steps to encourage Gen Y employees to stay longer at your company *without* paying us more money. The first step is to understand what your tenure cycles are saying and then add to this insight by uncovering why your employees actually leave. With this wealth of information you can determine the most appropriate way to address the patterns you uncover and measure your progress. Soon your retention rates will be on the rise (along with your Gen Y employees' enthusiasm), which gives you the perfect opportunity to start solidifying Gen Y's priceless employee loyalty. Unlocking our loyalty is the step in the *Y-Size* process where you begin to turn our short-term performance gains into a long-term competitive advantage.

Y-SIZE QUESTIONS

1. What is the average tenure for your top-performing Gen Y employees?
2. What are the top three reasons good employees leave your company?
3. What type of deferred compensation, benefit, or reward can you offer that you're not offering now?

CHAPTER 14

Lead Me to Loyalty

(So you hear, "Sure, my work is exhausting, but I would never leave this job. I love it here.")

On a plane from Atlanta to Austin, a bottling company executive told me a revealing story about building Gen Y employee loyalty. Fifteen years ago he'd started on the ground floor with his company, one of the largest in the United States. He was literally delivering bottled sodas, juices, and waters to dozens of stores on a delivery route. Even though he's now an executive with the same company and is responsible for over 450 employees, he never forgot where he started.

The day before Easter, one of his Gen Y delivery drivers came to him with a special request. He asked whether there was any way he could have Easter off work to spend time with his young children. The executive, who has children of his own, agreed to take over the shift *himself* to help out the young employee.

When the executive showed up at the first grocery store on the route dressed as a regular delivery driver, he began stocking the shelves just like the old days, but, he admitted, a little slower. After all, it had been 15 years since he had loaded and organized the bottles onto tightly stacked shelves.

Two Gen Y employees from his biggest competitor were doing the same thing nearby. They started giving him a hard time about how slow he was going. He gave them a little grief back, and soon they were talking while filling the shelves. At the end of the day, the three crossed paths again, and this time he told them what his real job was and why he was stocking the shelves instead of his employee.

Their demeanor instantly changed. They asked if he would take a few minutes to give them some career advice—and a job. They were ready to leave their current employer *on the spot* to work for a boss who would take an employee's shift so that he could be with his little kids on a holiday.

"I may be a little slow with the stocking," the exec told me, "but I know what your generation is looking for in order to be loyal to a company. They want to see that they're not just a number. That they can count on you." Indeed, not only did he win huge loyalty points from his current Gen Y employee, he also earned the loyalty (and job applications) from two of his competitor's employees!

EMOTIONAL CONNECTIONS, NOT PAYCHECKS

As you can tell from this story, Gen Y loyalty is based on an *emotional connection* to a company and its leadership, not a paycheck. This type of emotional connection is not built overnight but over time, which is why you must first retain Gen Y (as described in the previous chapter) to have a chance to build our loyalty. Retention only means how *long* you are keeping Gen Y employees, not necessarily that you've connected with us in a way that makes us want to stay through the good and bad times or when something better comes along (like an executive willing to pick up our shift on Easter).

You see the results of increasing our retention without building our loyalty when Gen Y employees who've been with you for at least 13 months jump ship to a different employer. This is particularly true if the other employer offered them the same or relatively the same amount of money (anything less than a 10 percent pay difference should catch your attention from a loyalty perspective).

The disparity between retention and loyalty will be most evident when the economy regains its strength, which it eventually will, because companies will start hiring again and top performers will start being heavily recruited by your competition. (Hint: they are the "secret admirers" connecting with us on Facebook, not our old eighth-grade sweethearts.) You will know you've successfully built Gen Y's loyalty, rather than solely increased our retention, when we receive higher-paying job offers, and we choose to stay with you anyway. In fact, at one company I visited, employee loyalty is such a strong part of their culture that employees tack the higher-paying job offers they receive to a wall in their office. Now *that* is loyalty— and a great homemade dartboard.

RECOGNIZE THAT EMPLOYEE AS MORE THAN STORE CLERK #8273A4

The emotional connection that develops into Gen Y employee loyalty isn't based on giving us an annual cost-of-living raise or a multiple hyphenated title (like Assistant-to-the-Assistant-of-the-Executive-Office's-Assistant). Those are steps that can increase our retention, which in turn gives you more opportunity to build our loyalty (and who doesn't want a title so long it covers both sides of your business card?). However, what Gen Y most wants in order to be a loyal employee is for you to value us as more than store clerk # 8273A4.

We want you to see us as an individual *first*, as Jason from Austin who likes Tex-Mex food and live music, and as your employee *second*. Once we feel that you appreciate us as individuals, *then* you've laid the foundation for us to create a safe emotional space where we can begin to trust you with our loyalty. Creating this emotional space is pivotal, because this vulnerability makes us willing to put our professional future in your hands—something we do not take lightly, given our belief that we will likely have many employers throughout our career. You can make this belief work in your favor by taking the *Y-Size* loyalty-building steps that other employers overlook and, in effect, creating an employment experience unlike any we've ever had *or expected*.

COMMUNICATION LEADS TO TRUST, TRUST LEADS TO LOYALTY

The first and most important *Y-Size* step to building our loyalty is open, honest communication. With this in mind, your style of communication with us should change as Gen Y moves ahead with our careers at your company. We start out expecting primarily one-way communication from leadership (i.e., you showing us how to do our job and us doing it—at least on the second try). Then as we advance in your company, we expect more two-way, open communication. After all, the longer we stay with your company, the more risk we're taking by assuming that you're consistently making the right decisions for the company and, consequently, our future. As part of that leap of faith, we want to know what company leadership is doing, and at least some of the reasoning behind your decisions.

From a communication standpoint, nothing cements Gen Y's trust and belief in company leadership as quickly and effectively as uncensored, one-on-one, or small-group conversations with them. These in-person exchanges make us feel valued, connected, informed, and noticed. These interactions also help Gen Y see for ourselves that our company leaders are "for real." They also validate the effort and sacrifice we are willing to put forth to help the company reach its goals (for example, working on our coveted Saturdays).

These interactions can be as informal as a small-group lunch with an executive or as formal as a semiannual presentation from leadership to talented Gen Y employees about where the company is headed. At the very least, the next time your business has an event or meeting with the founder, owner, or CEO in attendance, arrange for the high-profile executive to shake hands and answer a few unscripted questions from Gen Y employees (and no, we're not going to ask them about wearing boxer shorts or briefs—that important trivia is reserved for presidential candidates). All it takes is one photo of us shaking hands with the CEO or a pat on the back by the company founder to create a cherished memory and strong emotional connection to the company. (And yes, we'll send the photo to our mom.)

SITTING WITH THE CEO

This happened for one of my college friends who graduated at the top of her business school class and went to work for a well-known Fortune 500 company. This company conducted regional meetings every year, where the CEO presented his update and go-forward strategies to regional executives. In a major change from tradition, the company decided to open the meeting to its top-performing young professionals within each region. These Gen Y employees were invited to attend their regional meeting and sit at tables with their supervisors. The very best of them were invited to sit at a VIP table with the CEO, and at the age of 23, my friend ended up sitting at that exclusive table.

She later told me that the highlight of her first year at her first real job was not receiving a substantial signing bonus, a company car (complete with gas card!), an expense account, international travel, or her own sales territory. Instead, the highlight was being invited to sit at a table with her multibillion-dollar company's CEO and have him ask for her opinion on a new product.

At that moment her loyalty to the company soared—simply because he took two minutes to ask her opinion. This couldn't have come at a better time, because she was already considering other job offers. The additional cost to the company to invite her and other top-performing Gen Y employees to the regional meetings: a few extra helpings of banquet chicken and mashed potatoes. The payoff in Gen Y employee loyalty: priceless.

If it is simply impossible for your company to arrange for senior leadership to have occasional two-way communication with Gen Y employees, consider creating a monthly or quarterly leadership Q&A via technology. Ask young professionals to e-mail a specific company leader (or, more likely, that person's assistant) ahead of time with their questions. The company leader can then answer some of these questions via a Web conference, conference call, yammer.com, or some other internal network. Gen Y wants to know what our leaders are thinking, so let us ask them a few questions and feel as though we are privy to the conversation. A side benefit to this candid exchange is that senior leadership gains a direct pipeline into the perspectives, concerns, and priorities of their Gen Y employees (and without having to leave their corner office). Brilliant!

You reinforce the two-way communication that forms the backbone of Gen Y employee loyalty with smaller, authentic loyalty-building gestures. These gestures, planned or spontaneous, solidify our emotional connection to you and the company (and give us lots of things to Twitter about on the way home from work).

IF I CAN COUNT ON YOU, YOU CAN COUNT ON ME

When you stand by your Gen Y employees in tough times, we are inspired to do the same for you. At Roy's restaurant, a part-time waiter suffered a devastating accident outside of work. He would never be able to regain his physical independence. The general manager of the restaurant heard the tragic news and immediately asked his employees if they wanted to hold a fundraiser for their injured coworker. Every employee, from the chef to the dishwasher said, "Yes!" The general manager worked with friends of the injured Gen Y employee to plan the fundraiser and solicit items for a silent auction.

One month later, the fundraiser was held. The restaurant donated all the food. The employees donated their time and any tips they received. A local band played for free. More than 200 people showed up. (I was the one dancing out of rhythm in the corner.) At the end of the evening almost $25,000 was raised to help the injured part-time worker! The financial support could not have come at a better time, because the 30-year-old had no health insurance. Everyone who participated in the fundraiser was inspired by the outcome, and the general manager showed how he sticks by his employees in good times and tough times. This huge display of loyalty became the talk of our local restaurant industry.

At another company, one of the employees developed a serious medical condition requiring a lengthy hospital stay. The employee was at risk of losing her job because she was going to miss so much work due to the extensive treatment required. Her immediate supervisor sent an e-mail to all the coworkers in their division asking them if they would donate one vacation day toward their sick coworker. The sick employee received so many donated vacation days that she was able to complete the life-saving treatment and eventually return to work. When the CEO of the company heard what had taken place, he immediately reimbursed every employee *twice* the vacation days they had donated!

Few things leave as permanent an impression on employees as how an employer treats us when we're affected by trauma or tragedy (i.e., we *never* forget). When this happens, every leader can rise to the challenge to do something—no matter how small—to show your commitment to your employees' well-being. You can connect an employee to a medical specialist they otherwise might not be able to access, or you can act like my friend, Dan, who bought an airline ticket for a young employee whose father passed away unexpectedly. Can you imagine the emotion the employee felt when Dan stepped up to make sure he was able to be with his family during such an important life experience?

Outback Steakhouse knows how important it is to stand by employees in tough times. They have an emergency fund called "The Outback Trust," that employees can apply for in times of financial distress. The leadership at Outback Steakhouse started this fund to support employees who suffered significant financial setbacks not covered by insurance. Every year, each of their restaurants holds a fundraiser to support the fund, ranging from car washes and golf tournaments to personal $20 contributions. Since the fund's creation, they have supported thousands of Outbackers (employees), from victims of hurricanes and apartment fires to people with emergency medical requests. They have even continued paying employees when a restaurant had to temporarily close due to fire damage. Now that is a show of loyalty their employees won't soon forget!

KEEP IT IN THE FAMILY

Contrary to the image we like to project to our friends, Gen Y's greatest influence is not *American Idol* or *The Daily Show* but our family. When you as an employer connect in a meaningful way with our families, you've taken our loyalty to a new level. At the same time, you have made it much more difficult for us to quit without a very good reason (because if we quit and our mom doesn't like the reason, we may be without both a job *and* a place to live rent-free). The easiest way to initiate a connection with Gen Y's family is to offer some type of benefit for them to use your company's product or services.

If your business is a video game company, consider giving our families access to free video games or to beta-test versions before they are released. If your business is a fitness center, consider giving our immediate family members discounted or free memberships. Or if your business is a retail store, you might offer our family members discounted pricing on a designated Family Weekend each year. At the very least, whenever a Gen Y employee's family visits your business, make it a point to greet them and praise the employee *in front of his or her family.*

At some restaurant chains they achieve this family connection by having a Family Night twice a year. On this designated night, family members eat for free. Management also gives them a tour of the restaurant so that they can see where their family member works and why they are so important to the restaurant. Now that makes Mama proud (and gets her a side of fries)!

MAKE OUR WORK SPACE *OUR* SPACE— WITHIN REASON

Gen Y wants to feel that our work space is *our* space. This aligns with our desire to retain our individualism within a larger group. You can accommodate this desire by giving us a little flexibility in tastefully personalizing our workspace. To allow this flexibility without giving us room to go overboard (such as hanging up our favorite nude self-portrait), create a detailed list of what we can display at work. The list could include family photos, pet photos, children's art, graduation photos, client testimonials, professional awards or certificates, media articles, and items representing our alma mater. These photos, documents, and items make Gen Y feel that our work space is not "just a cubicle" or "just a workbench." It's now *our* cubicle or *our* workbench—*and we've hung up our 12th-place ribbon to prove it.*

These personal displays also give our bosses conversational clues to help them build stronger emotional bonds with us. For example, if you see pictures of us at a car show, you know you could talk with us about cars. The same goes if we have pictures of us enjoying a concert, skiing, playing volleyball, volunteering, or attending a sporting event. If customizing workspaces is not practical for your business environment, allow us to at least customize our nametag, locker, or some other personal space. You could also give us a vote in picking out new furniture or paint colors for the employee common areas. (Ahh, I see beanbags and spearmint walls!)

How important to Gen Y is the ability to make our own office space personal? A Boomer executive I met at an IT conference told me that he has always had a rule that employees could not display personal pictures in their workspace until they had been employed at least six months. He said this year he had to change the rule because his Gen Y employees were unwilling to wait that long! Makes sense to me. Can you imagine the trouble we'd be in if Mom came to visit and her picture was not on our desk?

REINFORCE THE POSITIVE

Gen Y is known as an optimistic generation (just ask us how soon we think we should get promoted). One tradeoff to our optimism is that we are quickly turned off when confronted with negative messaging. In many companies I visit—particularly those with employee-only break rooms and departments—I see news clippings, magazine cartoons, and photos displayed inside cubicles or tacked to walls that send a negative, offensive, or sarcastic message. While these may be humorous to the employee who posted them, they are absolutely unprofessional, disrespectful, and add an unnecessary negative vibe to your workspace. Get rid of these inspiration black holes.

You work hard enough to motivate your employees to do a good job and work as a unified team, so don't let some off-color political cartoon bring us down when we show up to work or take our lunch break. This is especially true for your sales and customer service employees, who need as much positive reinforcement as possible because they already deal with plenty of negativity. (Just listen in on one of their complaint calls and you'll know what I mean.) You can easily keep your office positive by enforcing a simple rule, which states that only positive messages and images that align with your company's core values are allowed to be posted anywhere in the company's offices.

CELEBRATE OUR MOST IMPORTANT HOLIDAY

What is the most important holiday to Gen Y? Our birthday. Why? Because it's the only holiday all about us! In fact, we don't just celebrate our actual birthday—oh no, we usually have a birthday weekend, a birthday week, and some of us pull off an entire birthday month. It's not May. It's Jason Month!

The significance of birthdays make them perfect times to strengthen our emotional connection to you and your company—and lift everyone's spirits. There are numerous ways to make our birthdays memorable without investing a lot of money or effort (although sometimes you just want to deflate the helium balloons yourself). The coolest birthday celebration I've seen was at a company that gives employees of all ages $50 on their birthday, along with a disposable camera or loaned digital camera. The birthday employees are instructed to use the money to do something that day that they've never done before—and take pictures while doing it. They are then to bring the pictures to work the next day and show everyone what they did.

Some of the birthday employees used the money toward big personal goals, such as skydiving, while others donated the money to charity and volunteered. One younger Gen Y employee took his wife to dinner. Apparently he'd never done that before (ouch). Other ideas I've seen that were a big hit on birthdays: Fill the person's office with balloons from floor to ceiling that so they have to pop the balloons to enter, have a theme party 10 minutes before work closes (Hawaiian is always popular), or buy a gigantic birthday card that every employee signs and then have the entire office sing them "Happy Birthday" while they are presented with the card and a birthday cupcake. All of these are better than asking every employee to chip in $5 for a cheesy card and a buffet lunch no one wants to attend.

MAKE A PERSONAL CONNECTION

Gen Y defines ourselves by what we do after 5 PM. Your company can use this insight to build our loyalty by supporting our non-work goals. All you have to do is ask your Gen Y employees for one non-work goal he or she wants to achieve each year and then find a small way to help him or her reach it. If we want to run a marathon, sponsor our number. If we want to learn to paint, give us a gift certificate to a painting class or art shop (it's better than us practicing in marker on the bathroom walls). If we want to climb Mount Everest, give us a subscription to a mountain climbing magazine. You can do each of these things randomly, or make it a tradition to show your support for one of our personal goals on an employee's first employment anniversary. Anything you can do to show you support us personally will be rewarded by greater commitment from us professionally.

CELEBRATE SUCCESS AND YOU'LL SEE MORE OF IT

Every week something good happens at your office or business—if you look for it. Even tiny steps forward represent progress (Yay! The phones worked the entire week!). Celebrating these successes, small and large, cultivates a results-driven culture and builds an emotional high point for that day or week. You also deliver the tangible outcomes and public recognition that Gen Y craves. My recommendation: Five-minute Success Celebrations. These are a fast, fun, and virtually free way to keep your employees motivated and outcome oriented.

If you have a strong sales week, hand out plastic badges so that people become the "Sheriffs of Sales." If you win an award, make the announcement standing on your desk or ring an oversized cowbell that then becomes the "Sound of Success." During these Five-minute Success Celebrations thank the people involved and specify why you are celebrating. These explanations highlight the actions and attitude you want to see more often in your office. To make the emotion from these celebrations last longer, take pictures and place the photos in your employee break room or reception area and post them on your company blog.

At an outpatient rehabilitation clinic, the company had finally reached a point where they needed to knock down a wall to add more space. They could have simply called in a construction crew to do the demolition, but, instead, they chose to make it a loyalty-building experience for the employees. Every employee was asked to sign his or her name in bright colors on the wall that was going to be knocked down. The employees could also make their handprint in paint or write something motivational directly on the wall. After everyone in the company had made their mark on the wall, each employee was given a sledgehammer and a chance to help knock down the wall. The more the dust went flying, the more everyone got excited. Once the wall was demolished, each employee was given a piece of the wall as a memento of "the barrier to growth they helped knock down."

I promise: The more you celebrate success, the more you'll start to see it.

CELEBRATE PERSONAL BREAKTHROUGHS, TOO

Personal breakthroughs are often the most meaningful to Gen Y, and we often want to share these, when appropriate, with our colleagues. One of my favorite ways to celebrate personal success at work is by designating a Brag Board. This is a corkboard where employees post achievements from their lives outside of work directly next to major company achievements. What you end up with is a major sales contract or industry award notification tacked next to an employee's kid's sixth-grade report card. Very cool.

If your employees do not share one physical location or a Brag Board won't fit your office, consider creating a virtual water cooler instead. Jonathan Davis, CEO of American Workforce, did this by creating an account with an online photo-sharing web site and asking his employees to upload photos and videos of their kids doing funny things. To keep it fun, employees came up with monthly themes to encourage creativity, like "First Day of Summer" and "Baseball, Apple Pie, American Workforce" and then empowered them to pick the prizes and vote on the winners. This has been a big hit in helping employees feel connected (and competitive) even though they work in different locations, and it's had the added benefit of being a great recruiting tool as well.

VOLUNTEER TO GIVE MORE AT WORK

Much research has shown that Gen Y finds great meaning in volunteering time to socially responsible causes. Your company can align with our desire for corporate social responsibility by providing regular avenues for us to support various causes through our employer and, ideally, volunteer with our coworkers. KeyStaff, an employee placement service, closes its entire office for one day each quarter to do some type of community service project. In the last year, they walked dogs (and "scooped poop") at their local animal shelter, volunteered at a nursing home, and even painted street curbs in an effort to improve their community. Not only do these quarterly service projects show KeyStaff's employees that the company is committed to helping its local community, but people like me look forward to seeing what the company has chosen to do this quarter (and checking out the funny pictures from their last project, which are included in their e-newsletter).

One of the coolest annual volunteer projects I've learned about is led by Lee Curtis, CEO of BridgeStreet, a large corporate housing company. At BridgeStreet's annual meetings, which include employees from around the world, everyone works together on a volunteer project. During their last annual meeting, all the attendees, from the CEO to the receptionists, worked together to clean up an inner-city park in Baltimore. What most inspired me was Lee saying to the attendees that the volunteer project is one of the most important things the company does each year. He feels it embodies everything BridgeStreet stands for in terms of making their communities great places to live.

From a Gen Y perspective, when we watch senior executives, like Lee, getting their hands dirty alongside the most junior employees, the message is clear: "This is important, and we're all in it together." At the same time, when people volunteer together they are creating a shared memory with a vivid emotional connection. For maximum impact, ask your senior leaders to serve food or distribute prizes to the employees when the volunteer event concludes. This act of service is a powerful exclamation mark on your commitment to be socially responsible.

If your business model makes it impossible for you to take a company-wide volunteer day, create other volunteer or socially responsible experiences. One option is to offer every employee one paid volunteer day per year. We get the paid day off work to make a difference in our community, but we also must take pictures of our efforts to show our coworkers. Another option is to host a day for students to shadow company employees or sponsor a more traditional canned food drive. Any steps that demonstrate your company's commitment to helping others will strongly resonate with Gen Y (and remind us why we like working in air conditioning).

ORGANIZE A GREEN TEAM

If you're looking for a volunteer effort that can really lead to more green, both for your bottom line and your community, organize a Green Team. This team of employees assesses where your company could improve its impact on the environment and save money. They review everything from your carbon footprint and landscaping to recycling and carpooling. They then make a list of Green Team recommendations for improvement, potential results from each recommendation, and the direct and indirect costs and savings associated with implementing each recommendation. Executives select one or two recommendations to implement each year. The Green Team then tracks the progress and presents the results on a regular basis. Once the results are documented they are shared with employees and customers, both of whom will be impressed by your efforts—especially Gen Y.

At Aveda, a natural cosmetics company with a long history of environmental responsibility, management is continually challenging employees to find ways to make the company more ecologically responsible. In pursuit of this goal, they have contests (such as one to raise money for Earth Month, which is their in-house effort to turn Earth Day into an entire month!). One employee decided to raise money by hand crafting two beautiful quilts using only vintage Aveda t-shirts. She then sold raffle tickets for the quilts and held a drawing to determine the winners. She ended up raising more money than any other employee. That could have been the end of the contest (and a positive one at that), but, for her contributions, Aveda awarded her with a company-sponsored eco-trip to Uganda to learn more about sustainable and organic partnerships. The employee was more inspired than ever and credits Aveda with one of the most memorable events in her life.

CREATE A VALUES VIDEO

To create an emotional connection between your company's core values and your employee's core values, consider making a Values Video. Stephen Shang, president of Falcon Storage, an on-site storage company, told me how he did this and how it played an important role in helping his company pull out of a financial crisis. The company had started losing money and the leadership team felt it was partly because the company had lost its alignment with its core values. To remind everyone about the significance of the company's core values, the leadership team organized an all-company meeting off site and divided the company into two teams.

Each team was instructed to make a video about Falcon showcasing the company's core values in action (service about self, integrity as defined by the Rotary Four-Way Test, self-motivation, strong sense of urgency, and individual responsibility). The employees were encouraged to use any props they could find at the meeting center, along with their own creativity. Both teams created their 10-minute Values Videos, which were broadcast to the entire company, accompanied by popcorn and tremendous audience applause (and a few bows from the video celebrities). The experience of making the videos helped bring the company back together, reinforced the importance of the company's core values, and created a pivotal point from which the company rebounded with tremendous growth.

Another variation on this concept is a *Why We Love This Place* video. Using a video recorder, go office to office (or cubicle to cubicle) recording various employees answering the same question: "Why do you love this place?" Some of the answers will be poignant, others hilarious, and in the end each one tells you something different about what makes your company great. Take the best answers and edit them together into a short video that shows why people are excited to work at your company. This one video will have more credibility with current and prospective employees than anything you can print.

ESTABLISH A HERITAGE HALLWAY OR VALUES WALL

If video production is not your cup of tea (or you have shaky hands), invest your efforts in some type of loyalty space, such as a Heritage Hallway or Values Wall. In these high-traffic areas of your workplace you send a visual message about what is most important at your company. On a Values Wall you can showcase initiatives (such as the Green Team), projects, successes, achievements (Volunteer of the Year) and photos that emphasize your company's values. These photos and other types of recognition should hang next to a list of your company's values signed by company leadership and employees. The most effective Values Walls bring your company values to life by demonstrating those values in action.

A Heritage Hallway takes a different approach by highlighting where your company comes from and where you're headed. This wall includes photos of your company's first office space, original products or services, historical photos or newspaper clippings, industry awards, and other company milestones. Included should be photos of top executives at their first job and current job. This is especially powerful if they worked their way up the ranks from an entry-level position or helped start the company. Either way, it sends the message to Gen Y that you can start at the ground level and work your way to the top.

GEN Y WANTS YOU TO BRING YOUR MISSION TO LIFE

Your company's mission is the "why" behind your company's existence. The more you bring your "why" to life, the more your Gen Y employees will *emotionally connect* with the outcomes your company creates. To build this emotional connection, focus on the results of the products and services you play a role in delivering. For example, if you sell life insurance, show how your insurance policy kept a family in its house at a most tragic time. You can do this by posting a thank you letter from the family and a picture of family members standing next to their house. If you design some type of alert technology, show the news coverage detailing how your technology saved a life by directing EMS to an accident hidden from view. If you're a grocery store chain, remind employees of the memories your food helps create at Thanksgiving. You can do this by sharing a note from a grandparent who used your groceries to create a memory she will never forget. Whatever your business, there is *always* a way to bring the impact of your products and services to life and in doing so remind Gen Y of your mission.

ABOVE ALL: BE UNPREDICTABLE

The biggest lesson I learned when it comes to emotionally reinforcing your loyalty-building efforts: *be unpredictable.* Invite the mayor for a tour of your business and brag about your employees in front of her; hand out goodie bags unannounced at 3 PM on a random Wednesday; have a marshmallow-eating contest before lunch; or pay someone to shine shoes for employees while we work. Your Gen Y employees may not know what you're going to do next, but we know it will be interesting and exciting, which makes us keep showing up to find out!

Y-SIZE QUESTIONS

1. How do you maintain two-way communication with your Gen Y employees?
2. What can you do to demonstrate to your employees that you are there for them in tough times?
3. When was the last time you did something unpredictable to emotionally connect with your employees?

CHAPTER 15

Build a Talent Pipeline Like *American Idol*

(Or, "I read on Facebook that this is the place to be!")

Once you've *Y-Sized* each step in the Gen Y employee life cycle—from attracting us (and our online friends) to building our emotional loyalty—you now have a chance to lock in your competitive advantage for the next five to seven years. You do this by positioning your company as *the place* for the best and brightest Gen Y minds to launch our careers when we're ready to work (with or without parental prompting). This means getting those of us who are not yet old enough or who are still pursuing advanced degrees to think of your company *first* when we are daydreaming about our ideal place of employment (usually around 3 PM in a statistics lecture).

Can you imagine the hiring advantage you have when the most sought-after Gen Y recruits receive your job offer along with three of your competitors, but your company is the only one they have had bookmarked on their computers for five years? At that point, it's not about the money. It's all about the *reputation* you've earned through a few *Y-Size* Talent Pipeline initiatives.

Yes, I realize that in this current economic environment some people are not nearly as concerned about having the right employees five years from now as they are about staying in business this year. I get it. However, I also know that despite the challenging economy, forward-thinking executives must keep their future workforce needs in mind if they are going to adequately address them. Otherwise, you will have to compensate down the line for your lack of preparation by paying more than your competitors to hire talented Gen Y employees or deal with the consequences of simply not having the employees you need to grow your business effectively.

When I was speaking with an executive at a large aerospace company, she made it clear to me that her company is actively working *today* to make sure it has the new hires it will need five years from now. Why? Because by acting now to *identify* and *embrace* those talented Gen Yers, the company will have a huge advantage over its competitors—the ones who didn't show up on the recruiting scene until the semester before graduation (and all they had to offer was free glow-in-the-dark keychains—how exciting).

This aerospace company, like many large companies, can also look at its current employee demographics and see that, even if revenues remain flat, it will still need to add a large number of new employees—many of whom will be members of Gen Y. This is particularly true in highly skilled industries such as healthcare, which will face an employee shortage when Boomers eventually decide to stop showing up to work early and staying so late.

Your goal in building a Talent Pipeline is straightforward: to establish a strong and visible reputation as an exciting, dynamic place where ambitious and talented Gen Y employees have the resources and leadership necessary to thrive. This is easier than it sounds. All you need are a few signature *Y-Size* initiatives that will build buzz around the opportunities you offer talented Gen Y employees.

To build your talent pipeline, I have pinpointed five initiatives that will help you identify and embrace emerging Gen Y talent— and do so in a way that benefits your current operations. You don't have to implement all five. Even one signature initiative can make a big difference in your future hiring efforts.

1. LAUNCH A PROJECT-BASED INTERNSHIP PROGRAM

Internships are one of my favorite ways to attract your next wave of talent while benefiting your current operations. The challenge with many internship programs is that they are structured in a way that is not exciting for the intern or particularly beneficial to the employer, which means that both end up disappointed. To make an internship valuable for you and the Gen Y intern, the key is to set expectations up front and to make it more than just the traditional paper-filing marathon.

Faith Taylor, worldwide vice president of sustainability and innovation for the Wyndham hotel group, told me about Wyndham's summer internship program, which spans all three of their corporate divisions and is largely project-based. Summer interns, all of whom are in Gen Y, are told ahead of time about the job and assignment expectations, and then they are given several projects along with ongoing responsibilities. One recent project was to create a business plan for Wyndham's flagship Green initiative. She said the interns were exactly the right people to tackle the Green initiative, because it has to connect with Gen Y on multiple levels—as community members, as employees, and as customers. She said the interns took the Green initiative project very seriously and came up with "awesome ideas," which the executive team evaluated and considered for integration into their operational strategies.

The best internships are much like the one Faith described. The companies offer interesting projects that are interactive and oucome-driven, and they have clear expectations for what their interns are to accomplish. To create this type of experience, start by focusing on projects and outcomes rather than on ongoing responsibilities. If your current internship structure is heavily focused on ongoing responsibilities, find projects within those responsibilities or add outcomes on a regular basis. Sure, there are going be assignments we have to tackle every day (such as picking up your favorite coffee on the way to work), but it's the projects and outcomes that make the internship valuable to everyone involved, including you as our boss.

Projects that an intern might take on include:

- Attempting to find a new solution to old problems facing the business (remember, younger interns don't know what you can't do, so we are able to focus on possibilities rather than feel limited by past experiences).
- Conducting research in support of an industry white paper.
- Grassroots marketing that leads to a presentation and portfolio.
- Creating a new blog, Wiki, Twitter feed, or other online presence for your company. (Gen Y is particularly well suited to take on any projects you have related to social media and its implications for your business.)
- Examining future projects or potential products and services based on company history and current trends.

You can also follow the lead of L-3 Enterprise IT Solutions, which combines the best of what Gen Y wants by offering a cross-functional, project-based internship. This approach enables interns to get tremendous exposure to the company's culture, see where they fit from an operational perspective, and complete several different projects *all in one summer.*

With this type of internship approach in mind, solicit applications by using the *Y-Size* strategies outlined earlier in this book, and by partnering with an appropriate educational institution. This could be a local university, two-year college, or high school career and technology department. Keep in mind that the earlier you can provide Gen Y with a great work experience, the easier it will be to turn that experience into a future employment relationship.

One thing I've noticed at many four-year colleges is that the vast majority of internships are only to available to upperclassmen. When it comes to building your talent pipeline, use this knowledge to your advantage by taking the opposite approach and opening your internships to first- and second-year students. They have fewer internship options, which means you will draw a more talented pool of applicants who will also be more motivated to prove themselves.

When you offer your internships in partnership with an educational institution, ask about offering the internship for credit. This adds a nice enticement to attract the best interns to your company, and it also makes it even more in their interest to do an excellent job for you. Sometimes earning credit for an internship can also result in the intern working for free, as long as you turn in a regular evaluation to their teacher or professor. Now *that* is a win/win; we gain credit for real-world learning, and you gain a talented employee at a very attractive cost basis (i.e., free).

However you choose to approach your project-based internship, there are a few steps you should always take to make sure it goes well:

- *Market your internship to the highest concentration of potential interns.* Unlike full-time jobs, word does not spread as fast or as far when it comes to internships. The best way I've found to address this is to have someone from your company (ideally someone close to the age of potential interns) speak directly to a class or to classes of students who are studying a subject that dovetails with your business or industry.

In this presentation, share what makes your internship exciting and different, as well as the outlook for career advancement within your business for the next few years. If you can't speak to classrooms of potential interns, participate in your local high school, college, or community career fair, and contact the appropriate departments to see if they will internally publicize the internship. You can even market your internship as a prize for the winner of a college's business plan contest or some other business-related competition.

- *Allow potential interns to submit their applications and answer a few nontraditional questions* (such as those detailed earlier in the *Y-Size* process). Intern applicants usually have even less work experience than full-time applicants, so these off-the-wall questions will really intrigue them about your opportunity.
- *Start the internship with clear expectations on both sides, preferably in writing.* Share exactly what you expect from your interns—ranging from punctuality and attire to asking for help and cell phone etiquette. Be specific about what you are offering them in return. Hot buttons to definitely mention include lunches with management, a strong recommendation if they do a good job, and being able to attend some kind of community event with our boss.

- *Deliver specific constructive feedback to your interns on a weekly basis.* If possible, present this to us in writing. Gen Y needs regular feedback and guidance, especially when we are first entering the workforce.

If you're unable to have interns for an extended period of time, such as a semester or the entire summer, consider hosting a Real World Challenge instead. In a Real World Challenge, you partner with a college, technical school, or high school. Your education partner provides you with up to three prescreened Gen Y students who are interested in the world of business and in learning how to succeed faster. This team of students arrives at your business on a Monday morning wearing appropriate business attire.

Upon arrival, they are presented with an actual problem facing your business and have five days to try to solve it. They do their own research and can interview employees and anyone else you designate. On Friday afternoon of the same week that they began the Challenge, the team presents their solution to company leadership. This is a great way to identify talented employee prospects early on and get a different perspective on an actual challenge facing your company (for free!).

Whatever strategy you use to attract your interns, the more project-based, hands-on, and creative the internship, the deeper the connection you will make. This connection will allow you to identify and embrace the Gen Yers who will grow to become your talent pipeline and, if you stay in contact with them, future employee superstars.

2. SUPPORT YOUNG PROFESSIONALS ASSOCIATIONS

Young Professionals Associations, also called YPAs, are one of the only places where employers can reach a large and concentrated group of Gen Y young professionals after college graduation. However, many employers overlook these associations and instead head to their Rotary luncheon so that they can hear the mayor speak for the 57th time. Well, it's time to loosen the tie, forego the buffet line, and meet the young professionals in your community who are going places—hopefully, to work for your company.

Depending on the size of your community, you may have several YPAs to choose from, so I recommend finding the one that has members who best fit your company and its culture. This could be a community-wide Young Professionals Association, a statewide YPA geared toward your industry, or some regional organization with a shared characteristic, like a forum for young professionals.

For example, where I live we have a program called Leadership Austin. This is a highly regarded (and extremely selective) program where gaining admission means experienced community leaders feel you have the potential to make a significant contribution to our community. As an employer, getting in front of a group like Leadership Austin presents a valuable opportunity to reach the best and the brightest *who already live in the area* all at one time and in a setting that is conducive to dialogue.

If there are no Young Professionals Associations in your community, consider providing resources and leadership to start one. If your community already has a prominent YPA (or several), consider sponsoring or creating an award recognizing a young professional who embodies the mission or values that your company is all about. These awards, often given names like "30 under 30," showcase a concentration of talent and attract other up-and-comers who want to win the awards. The relationships and visibility you develop by supporting young professionals associations not only will help build your talent pipeline but can also convince young professionals to make the jump to your team *now*. After all, you're the selection committee for the award they want to win.

3. SHOWCASE YOUR COMMUNITY AS A COOL PLACE TO LIVE

Gen Y moves to a new city and *then* looks for a job. While logically this drives our parents crazy, it makes many a moving company happy. You can use this insight to help build your talent pipeline by attracting talented Gen Yers to your community who will ultimately be in search of employment (at least once mom, or Visa, cuts us off). Once we've made the geographic move, you can use the other *Y-Size* steps to make your business *the* place to work within your community. Essentially you want a talented Gen Yer to show up in your community, $2,000 laptop in hand, and turn to one of our six new roommates and say,

"So, where is the coolest place to work around here?" and have the roommates point in your company's direction.

While rebranding an entire community is easily a thick book (or three) by itself, there are a few simple things that an individual employer or group of employers can do. The easiest is to create a web site dedicated to Gen Y in your community. On this web site, provide a calendar of cool upcoming things Gen Y might want to attend (festivals, concerts, shopping events, outdoor competitions, etc.). Also, include a place for Gen Yers already living in your community to blog about things going on in your city from their point of view (or have a RSS feed from their blog to your community web site). Build on this user-generated content by asking Gen Yers to post pictures, videos, and tweets from events happening in your city that are likely attractive to our peers—whether that is something like Flugtag or simply a Friday night on the town. Gen Y is hugely attracted to places we see as "happening," so let us see the action for ourselves.

In addition to having individuals post to your Gen Y community site, ask local and regional social clubs, civic groups, educational institutions, and nonprofits to add their own highlights and latest adventures. You want to bring the flavor and vitality of your community to the Web, so that Gen Y gets what your community is all about and wants to become part of the mix.

I also recommend that you provide several fun lists such as "Ten Reasons To Move Here (Without Telling Your Mom), Five Things To Do If You Only Have Five Hours In Our Town, and Twenty Things To Do For Free When You Visit." These resources should align with the Gen Y hot buttons described earlier in the book, such as lifestyle, food, festivals, dating, recreation, and assorted other fun. The more lakes, coffee shops, hiking trails, entrepreneurship boot camps, and beer crawls you can showcase (or Twitter from while crawling), the faster we will show up in your town, ready to join the fun *and find a job.*

Using these same Web elements, create a Facebook group or other social network group specifically for Gen Yers in your community. By connecting your Gen Y community with a social network (or five) it's much easier for current Gen Y residents to promote your community as a cool place to visit and live because we can simply add it to our profile. For a listing of communities that are actively engaging Gen Y through the Web and social networks, visit www.ysize.com/ch15.

4. RECRUIT GEN Y WITH GEN Y

Gen Y trusts our peers more than almost anyone else (except maybe Google). Make this a recruiting advantage for your company. Train your current Gen Y employees to become peer-to-peer recruiters. We don't have to know everything about your company (or even the difference between an exempt and non-exempt employee); our enthusiasm, honesty, and baby faces will work wonders. If you recruit heavily from a certain college or handful of colleges, consider offering workshops by your employees as a learning resource to students via professors and student organizations.

You do this by creating two or three 30-minute workshops that align with your company's core values or operations, such as professionalism, customer service, creativity, and so on. These 30-minute workshops could have three or four key points and might be led by employees who recently graduated from the university where they will be speaking.

By offering these workshops as a free resource, you can get in front of entire classes and student organization meetings without positioning yourself as a recruiter. This not only gives you concentrated face time with large groups of students, it's also a lot less stressful than hosting a career fair booth (and giving away 300 flashing pens so that we stop and talk). At the same time, the workshops are a great community service. They also build the peer-to-peer relationships that Gen Y values tremendously when we are trying to figure out the right place to start our careers.

Continuing with this peer-to-peer strategy, ask your Gen Y employees to e-mail their friends (particularly those still in school or college) about recruiting events or sponsor a "friends and family" party at your office. These parties are particularly useful because they give a prospective Gen Y hire a chance to check out your company firsthand and see for themselves how cool it would be to work for you (and on the same floor with their best friend). If a current Gen Y employee ends up referring a peer that you hire, give that employee a reward when the new hire stays *for a full year*.

5. CONVINCE PARENTS OF GEN Y THAT THEIR KIDS SHOULD APPLY

This is probably my most controversial approach for building a Gen Y talent pipeline, but it fits the reality of a generation whose parents "edited" our college essays (which is pretty amazing, considering some of us never saw the first version). You do this by sending information about your job opportunities directly to the parents of current college or technical school students within a certain geographic area that fits your hiring pattern.

You can also sponsor some type of parent day at the college, or go as far as to create a Parent Resource Office (or at least a specific e-mail address for parents of potential job applicants). You can even post a sign in your retail business that says "Parents: Want your kid to get a job? Please give them one of our job applications. We're looking for talented employees to help us better serve you!" Gen Y's parents have been involved in every facet of their kids' life, and getting a job is something they take seriously—especially since they cosigned on our college loans.

CREATE THE BUZZ FOR YOUR COMPANY

I know that taking the steps necessary to build a talent pipeline requires the belief that you will need good employees five years from now, but for many employers that is a leap well worth taking (and simply prudent). The real dividends from your Talent Pipeline efforts will not only be the Gen Yers you directly attract through project-based internships and the like, but the buzz you create within the Gen Y community as your company becomes *the* place to work. After all, you don't want to hire every Gen Yer. You just want to be the top choice for the best ones.

Y-SIZE QUESTIONS

1. Does your company have a project-based internship program?
2. What young professionals associations does your company support?
3. Have you considered presenting your employment opportunity to the parents of Gen Y?

A CALL TO ACTION: WHY REACH OUT TO GEN Y—YOUR LEGACY AND OPPORTUNITY

All around you is an incredible opportunity. We are an opportunity that's texting, typing, talking, and walking—and probably all at the same time. We are your opportunity to make *an entire generation* of 79.8 million people a competitive advantage for your company *and your career.*

Gen Y, my own generation, is entering the workforce in droves (and sometimes driven by our parents). Along with a few characteristics you probably find annoying (such as writing in parentheses in a compound sentence), we also bring many valuable skills and talents to your workplace—as well as a strong desire to make a difference for you, our employer.

The *Y-Size* strategies and actions shared in this book will help you to make the most of everything positive we bring to the workforce and address the areas where we can most benefit from your help. All that is missing now is for *you* to champion the belief that Gen Y employees can add value to your company and its culture, now and in the future.

We want, maybe even need, for you to take the *Y-Size* steps described in this book so that you can influence how other leaders at your company think about and manage us. We're not asking for a ribbon or a handout; *we're just asking for a chance*—a chance to prove that we can make a difference in the workplace and to demonstrate our potential to ourselves and to our families, not to mention our 4,637 friends on Facebook.

The catalyst for reaping the rewards of the *Y-Size* process is having at least *one person* within a company recognize the huge upside potential for better employing us and acting accordingly. I think the risk/reward is obvious, and I hope by now you do, too. I hope you will be that catalyst.

The right place to start *Y-Sizing* at your company is the step in your employee life cycle that demands your most urgent attention. Once you see results from *Y-Sizing* that step, then you can circle back and focus on the remaining steps. Taking this approach will give you an immediate, tangible return on your efforts. It will also win you support and momentum for more ambitious *Y-Size* steps. The key is to start wherever you are *now* and with whatever resources you can allocate so that you can begin systemically moving your Gen Y employees toward the performance you need to win in our challenging, global economy.

You will know *Y-Sizing* has taken root in your company's culture when you naturally attract and hire more quality Gen Y applicants with less effort, achieve better workplace performance from us faster, and keep us around longer to fill more job openings internally. By acting now, you gain an important head start on your competition in advance of a changing economic and labor landscape. You can also expect to position yourself for at least a five-year advantage, and possibly more, since the generation after us will have many similarities to Gen Y (plus an even shorter attention span and, yes, more confusing clothing and worse music).

When I think of the impact you can have on your company by taking the *Y-Size* steps outlined in this book, I can't help but recall my first "real" job. I had just turned 18 and moved to a new city where I didn't know anyone but my dad (on whose 1980's living room couch I was crashing). Upon my arrival, he told me I had 48 hours to get a job if I was going to continue staying with him, so I drove my $500 car to the closest well-lit restaurant I could find, Macaroni Grill, and applied for a job. Even though I'd had several jobs before, I'd never formally applied for one. My other jobs were "interview only," so this was the first one where I went through every step of the employee life cycle (including the fear of rejection).

My most vivid memory from the experience was the restaurant manager congratulating me on having landed a job as a busboy and then telling me that I would have to wear a tie *every* day. I couldn't believe people still wore ties to work—and to clear other people's dirty dishes! My reaction must not have been a surprise, because the manager promptly handed me a paper diagram showing how to tie a tie, and then he explained each step involved. Sure, previous generations learned how to tie a tie with their dad in front of a big mirror. Me, I learned as a busboy practicing in the parking lot of a restaurant along a major highway. (But my dad was so impressed with my new-found skill that he had me tie all his ties and hang them in his closet for future use.)

Last year, I returned to that same Macaroni Grill. The smell of fresh-baked bread still hung in the air. Sitting at one of their butcher paper-covered tables 13 years later, eating alone (at least that hadn't changed), I couldn't help but recall the excitement, fear, and sense of uncharted responsibility I felt when I first wandered inside the heavy wood doors looking for a job at age 18. *That first real job changed my life.* While I can't tell you my old manager's name, I can tell you that the skills I learned under his supervision were as meaningful to me as any I went on to learn completing case study after case study in business school.

At my first real job, I learned to deal with difficult people (coworkers and customers), to work under pressure with a diverse team, to be held accountable for the outcomes I created (which were more than one broken plate), and of course to tie a tie while sitting in an overheating car. Without a doubt, that first manager changed my life. Not only did he give me a job when I desperately needed one, he also gave me a chance to start learning what it takes to be successful in the real world.

You have the same opportunity to have a lasting impact on your Gen Y employees, whether we are just finishing high school or five years out of graduate school. We *all* have something to learn, and I hope you see that as a strategic opportunity for your company and a potential legacy for yourself.

ACKNOWLEDGMENTS

Writing this book has been a team endeavor—along with lots of solo time typing feverishly at Dominican Joe's coffee shop in Austin, Texas. There are a handful of people without whom this book simply would not be possible. First and foremost I want to thank my wife, Denise, who graciously gave up our dining room table for me to use when my favorite coffee shop was closed. Denise read countless versions of this manuscript and was the unwavering calm during my storm of deadlines. Thank you, my love. I'm so blessed that you're my best friend.

The second person I'd like to thank is my writing collaborator, Digby Diehl. Together we literally bridged the generations: him correcting my grammar (as only a Boomer can), and me teaching him new abbreviations for text messaging. Digby, you are a consummate professional and a skilled wordsmith who I know could have made this acknowledgment sound much, much better. Thanks to you and to your wife, Kay, for your dedication and belief in this project (and for Kay: Go Lakers!).

I'd also like to thank my outstanding literary agent, Nena Madonia. Nena, you are amazing. Thanks to you and the Dupree Miller agency for making this book a reality.

To Shannon Vargo and your colleagues at Wiley: Thanks for seeing the potential for companies to Y-Size their business!

Special thanks goes to my family and friends for their patience as I fell off the electronic grid in order to finish this book. Mom, you rock. Thanks for telling me my manuscript was good from the very beginning (even before it was written). You have always believed in me, and I appreciate you loaning me a credit card "for emergencies" back when I was 17. I promise to return it soon.

Dad, I know you think I'm still not working hard enough, but I promise I will have a callus on my hand sometime soon. I look forward to losing many more of your expensive golf balls!

Thanks also to John, Alanna, and Randy for always standing by my side. I know I can count on you and it means the world to me. And to my ESF group: Thanks for pushing me to my entrepreneurial limits (and then some). To my mentors: Thank you for your insight, your inspiration, and most of all your steadfast support. You make me strong.

A special debt of gratitude goes to my mentor and friend, Cam Marston. Cam, thank you for sharing your insights into the different generations in the workplace. Any organization would be fortunate to benefit from your expertise.

Finally, I'd like to thank all the executives, managers, and entrepreneurs who graciously allowed me to enter their businesses and ask lots of questions (which were not always easy to answer). I value your trust and look forward to many more conversations.

ABOUT THE AUTHOR

Jason Ryan Dorsey, The Gen Y Guy®, is an acclaimed keynote speaker, bestselling author, and award-winning entrepreneur. A well-known generational expert, Jason has been featured on *60 Minutes, 20/20, The Today Show, The View*, and in *Fortune* magazine. His talent is teaching business leaders creative and inexpensive ways to maximize Gen Y employee performance while increasing the value of all four generations in the workplace.

Jason's nontraditional path began when he authored his first book, *Graduate to Your Perfect Job*, at age 18. This book became a national bestseller and is estimated to have helped 100,000 members of Gen Y enter the workforce. Jason followed the success of his first book with three more, including *My Reality Check Bounced!*

In recent years, Jason's speaking, research, and consulting have focused on identifying and developing specific strategies and cost-effective actions for making a multigenerational workforce a competitive advantage. A proud member of Gen Y (who text messages his mom every day), Jason has delivered over 1,800 keynote speeches to audiences as large as 13,000, both across the United States and as far away as Egypt, Finland, Spain, and India. The cornerstones of his results-driven presentations are his high-energy delivery and his step-by-step actions that attendees can use immediately.

In recognition of his business achievements, Jason won the Austin Under 40 Entrepreneur of the Year Award at age 25—one of the youngest winners ever.

To learn more about Jason, request a customized speaking or consulting proposal, or watch his newest videos, please visit www.JasonDorsey.com or www.YSize.com.

INDEX